NINETY
PERCENT
MENTAL

NINETY PERCENT MENTAL

An All-Star Player Turned
Mental Skills Coach Reveals
the Hidden Game of Baseball

BOB TEWKSBURY

AND SCOTT MILLER

Da Capo Press

Da Capo Press
Hachette Book Group
1290 Avenue of the Americas, New York, NY 10104
www.dacapopress.com
@DaCapoPress

Printed in the United States of America
First Edition: March 2018

Published by Da Capo Press, an imprint of Perseus Books, LLC, a subsidiary of Hachette
Book Group, Inc. The Da Capo name and logo is a trademark of the Hachette Book Group.

The Hachette Speakers Bureau provides a wide range of authors for speaking events.
To find out more, go to www.hachettespeakersbureau.com or call (866) 376-6591.

The publisher is not responsible for websites (or their content) that are not owned by
the publisher.

Editorial production by Christine Marra, *Marra*thon Production Services.
www.marrathoneditorial.org

Book design by Jane Raese
Set in 11-point Archer

Library of Congress Cataloging-in-Publication Data has been applied for.
ISBN 978-0-7382-3378-9 (hardcover); ISBN 978-0-7382-3493-9 (ebook)

LSC-C

10 9 8 7 6 5 4 3 2 1

To the three people who make my world complete;
my son, Griffin, and daughter, Jenna, who give me joy,
happiness and endless love. I am so very proud of you both!
And the best teammate a man could ever have,
my amazing wife, Laura, who has been a continued source
of strength and love for over thirty years.
Here's to thirty more! I love you.

—BOB TEWKSBURY

For my wife, Kim, and daughter, Gretchen, who keep me going.
For my parents, Alan and Rosemary, who got me going.

—SCOTT MILLER

CONTENTS

Prologue

I am standing atop a desert mountain, I am starting a brand-new job and I am bleeding profusely.

At this moment, there is only one thing I am thinking with any reasonable degree of certainty, and that one thing is a bit of a problem:

I am about to die.

Well, as we say in the game, the great thing about baseball is that every single day, you have a chance to see something you've never seen before.

Oh, sure, hundreds of people safely hike Camelback Mountain near Phoenix, Arizona, every year. Many of them even make it all the way up and then all the way down again without even lugging back a patch of souvenir cactus needles sticking out of their skin.

Today, I am not one of those people. I am stuck, things are getting dicey and I already can close my eyes and visualize one of tonight's lead stories on MLB Network television: *New San Francisco Giants mental skills coach and former major league pitcher Bob Tewksbury met his demise today when…*

And to think, this all started innocently enough, with a phone call from San Francisco Giants general manager Bobby Evans three months earlier. Over the next several days we talked, questions were asked, philosophies were discussed, arrangements were made, a contract was signed. Now, here we were in the spring of 2017, and talk about a change in altitude. For the first time since 1999, I was employed by a major league baseball club other than the Boston Red Sox.

The finality of the big move really hit when I boarded the plane on that mid-February day headed west to Arizona instead of south to Florida. I was eager for the change in scenery, both literal and metaphorical, especially because I could see so many similarities between San Francisco and Boston, the place where I had become so comfortable over most of these past two decades.

There, we won World Series titles in 2004, 2007 and 2013 with a great core group of homegrown players like Dustin Pedroia, Jacoby Ellsbury, Kevin Youkilis, Xander Bogaerts, Jon Lester, Jonathan Papelbon and Clay Buchholz.

Here, they won three World Series in five years with a great core group of homegrown players like Buster Posey, Madison Bumgarner, Matt Cain, Brandon Crawford, Brandon Belt and Joe Panik. Leading this band of brothers was Bruce Bochy, surely a Hall of Fame manager one day and a skipper I knew well after pitching for him in San Diego in 1996.

It took a few days to get settled into a new routine, and the strange sensation of wearing the orange and black of the Giants instead of the red and blue of the Red Sox was the least of it. But each day got better and, daily, driving to my apartment in Scottsdale, I had a clear view of Camelback Mountain to the west. It is the most prominent landmark in the area, 2,707 feet in altitude and about five miles from the Giants' minor league complex, appropriately named due to a profile that resembles the hump and head of a kneeling camel.

Admiring that beautiful sight daily, I was intrigued enough to ask Dave Groeschner, the Giants' longtime head trainer, about the mountain. He gave me the lowdown: popular hiking spot, and occasionally both major and minor league players run the mountain for conditioning. "Is it difficult?" I asked. "Not so much," Groesch told me. "It's okay as long as you stay on the trail. But every year, a lot of people wind up getting airlifted off the mountain because of dehydration or injury."

"If you go up there, Tewks, make sure you stay on the path," Groesch reiterated.

Now, I'm not really a hiker, although I do like to walk. Maybe the former is evident from the fact that I laced up my new Nike turf shoes that day after our short, early spring workout, pulled on my Giants spring training–issued shorts and conditioning T-shirt, failed to tell anyone I was going on a hike and proceeded to take on a mountain, alone, that I knew nothing about. It couldn't be that difficult, could it? People of all ages hike Camelback. I parked, grabbed my phone in the unlikely event I would need it, snagged a bottle of water and breathed in the arid desert air. There are two different entry points to Camelback Mountain: Cholla and Echo. The "easier" hike, I was told, was the Cholla Trail. So off I went.

En route, I stopped to read the information posted on the big sign at the trailhead: no pets (check), bring water (check), get off the mountain before dark (check, it was only 3 P.M.) and stay on the path (got it). Maybe here is where I should mention I don't like heights. Flying, I've become accustomed to. But even driving on tall bridges gives me the shakes. Put me in a glass elevator standing next to the back panel and I stop breathing and must look the other way. Nevertheless . . . *Stay on the trail and all will be good.* It wasn't long before I got some elevation, which provided some fabulous views of the valley, my new spring home. As I hiked higher, I got a little anxious but simply kept my head down and kept going, looking up just to take in the view here and there. The sights were amazing. The trail wasn't crowded, and a couple ahead of me finally stopped to turn back and head down the mountain. Hmmm, was this the summit? Nah, can't be, can it? I decided to keep going until I came to a point in the trail that left me unsure of which way to go. Nobody was around to ask, or to follow. As I scanned the area, it looked like the path was straight ahead. I think now that perhaps that's another key rule of hiking. If you're unsure whether you should be going in a particular direction, you probably shouldn't.

So I hiked, the path narrowed, I hiked, the path narrowed even more, I hiked and . . . whoa, about eighteen hundred feet up in the air, looking out over greater Phoenix, it is utterly spectacular. The entire valley sprawls out below me. The iconic Phoenician golf course and resort is directly at the base of the mountain. In the distance, I see Tempe and Arizona State University. To my right, I see the big, domed football stadium in Glendale, home of multiple Super Bowls, and other parts west. And about sixty or seventy feet above me to my right is what I think is the top of the mountain. *Man, I'm this close. I think I should hike a little bit farther.* In my head I begin to hear a friendly and familiar voice. It's my dear friend Dan Luker, who we all know as "Adventure Dan." He was a hockey player at Hamilton College in Clinton, New York, a huge Boston Bruins fan and today continues to play hockey into his sixties. He's one of those guys you probably have in your group of friends, too; the one always up to take a risk. Swim with sharks? *Why not, it'll be fun!* Kayak around the jetty at Wells Beach back home in Maine in the middle of a blinding rainstorm with high winds? *It'll be fun!* This voice filling my ears, I put my head down and climb a bit farther. Yep, as I tell the players I coach, it's amazing how far you can travel when you have a goal and focus on the next step. Adventure Dan wouldn't stop now, and despite the slope of the terrain, a few more rocks and cacti and, heck, maybe even a snake or two, I wouldn't either. I was almost there.

Finally, far enough, I figure I'd better turn around. I didn't want to be like those losers my new head trainer was telling me about who had to be helicoptered off the mountain. So I turn around . . . surely this was the path back and . . . wait, *where* is the path? Somehow, back who knows how many steps, I had edged off of it.

Well. I know I have to go east, which is staying to my left, and knowing this I am quite sure I will merge back onto the path I somehow exited any moment now. As I hike, though, I do not see any path. As my heart begins to race, I pause for a moment of rational thought. *Okay,* I tell myself, *retrace your steps. Go back to where you were and take another look for the path.* So as I start to do that, *wham!* There is an excruciating pain in my right thigh. I look down and, shit, a six-inch cactus needle is thoroughly embedded in my leg. I reach for it, thinking I can just pull it out, but no dice. Turns out, it ain't that easy. In pain, I ponder my next move. I decide to use my new Nike turf shoe as a crowbar. Just do it, right? I sit on a nearby rock, place the inside of my shoe under the ends of the hundred or so cactus needles stuck into my thigh and yank. And . . . it is like ripping off a Band-Aid that has been superglued to any body part with hair. Ouch! As my thigh bleeds, I am thinking, *Is this thing poisonous? And if it is, how much time do I have to get down the mountain?* My body starts to feel funny. Poison? I gulp some water. My right thigh finally stops bleeding, but there are still so many cactus needles stuck in my skin.

My inner voice—that voice inside all of us, the one I call the Little Man, its benefits and detriments soon to be detailed in these pages by myself and players I've worked with like Anthony Rizzo, José Iglesias and others—now is bashing me pretty good. *How the hell did you get into this situation? You are going to be airlifted off of this mountain, aren't you? Nice way to start a new job, you idiot!* Now, my focus isn't so much on finding the main path as it is on the ledge I notice roughly seventy-five feet in front of me that seems to be getting closer. The path and angle I am taking down the mountain? It actually is taking me closer to this ledge. This is the point where my thoughts begin to turn from the whole embarrassing idea of not being airlifted off of the mountain to the survivalist notion of simply not dying on this mountain. I am becoming afraid I will lose my footing and slide closer to the ledge. I begin to think of how my wife, son and daughter will take the news. Seriously and literally, I have never felt so afraid of dying in my life. I tell myself, *Pull it together, Bob!* I climb a bit higher to gather my thoughts when, instead, I gather more cactus needles. Another attack of the jumping cholla, which I later (of *course* it would be later) learn is the most feared and hated cactus in the southwest desert. The pads easily separate from the main stem, the spines easily attach to your skin, clothes, shoes, whatever. This plant is covered with spines that are very difficult to get hold of and dislodge once they've got you. The jumping cholla plays dirty. The spines naturally curve once they pierce your skin, becoming, in a sense, reverse barbs, making them hell to remove. This time, they are embedded in my left ankle, and now I am feeling overwhelmed, scared and stupid.

Everything would have been fine had I just stayed on the path, like Groesch had warned. I find another rock, sit, remove the shoe from my left foot and again start pulling the cholla needles from my body. Wearing nonsupportive turf shoes instead of hiking shoes, I also take note that my left ankle is beginning to ache.

Mind racing, I know I must slow it down. Regrouping, the realization sinks in. What I need to do to escape this predicament is to employ the same mental skills techniques I used on the mound during my eighteen seasons pitching in professional baseball—thirteen in the big leagues—and the ones I've taught for more than a decade as a coach. Slow down ... breathe ... positive self-talk (hello again, Little Man) ... focus on the task at hand. Mistakes happen when people are tired and hurried.

Sitting on that rock, I know if there's one constant in life, it is that at various checkpoints we all find ourselves smack in the middle of situations in which we're tired and hurried, and navigating through this maze to successfully exit at the other end is not an easy proposition. These challenges spring up both in our work life and in our home life, often at the most stressful or inconvenient times, and it is vital both to sharpen and maintain the skills needed to conquer these obstacles.

Slow down ... breathe ... focus ...

CHANGING JOBS is one of the most stressful things a person ever does, be it a player joining a new team or you joining a new company. I had plenty of time to reflect on so much of this during the winter, an off-season that started too early for those of us in Boston when the red-hot Cleveland Indians eliminated us in a three-game AL Division Series sweep that nobody saw coming. A silver lining was that one of the favorite players I've ever worked with was establishing himself as a hero that October as the Indians, their own drought overshadowed by that of the Chicago Cubs, attempted to win their first World Series title since 1948.

Andrew Miller, Cleveland's intimidating relief ace, is a genuine, kind and humble person who always was very engaged in working to make himself better every day. Even during his early struggles, when he and I worked so hard together with the Red Sox from 2011 to 2014, he had a level of confidence in that one day those hard times would all be in his past. His willingness with the Yankees in New York and then with Terry Francona's Indians to pitch in whatever role was needed revealed the type of character this man has, and that has not changed with success. When I see him now, I see a man who is first a dad and a loving husband who happens to be a stud in the bullpen. I am in awe of his ability, proud and very happy for him and his success.

When the Red Sox–Indians Division Series started, long before the Giants and Camelback Mountain were anywhere near my radar, I had neither seen nor texted with Andrew since his midseason trade from the Yankees to the Indians, and I very much looked forward to seeing him when the series opened in Cleveland. I did see him, but very briefly, just outside the visitors' clubhouse after the Indians' 6-0 Game 2 win, as he was leaving Progressive Field. We didn't get to talk much, just a quick hello during which I told him he looked great and asked how his son, Max, was doing. One more game, in Boston, and the series was over in what seemed like the blink of an eye. I was really hoping to talk more with him in person, but clinch games pretty much prevent those conversations from happening. So I did the next best thing. I sent him a text, which led to the following exchange:

TEWKS: You look so composed and under control each pitch . . . very cool to see. No doubt you will be used a lot in the next series.

ANDREW: Thanks, I appreciate it. I was trying to look that way on the outside but the inside was a mess. Hopefully a bit easier next round.

TEWKS: I would be happy to talk about the inside stuff if you want . . . would be great to catch up.

ANDREW: Ya I think it's mostly playoff adrenaline. Need to channel it and slow down a bit more—I think mostly experience is the cure.

TEWKS: Breathe, take your own timeouts to reset. 2-0, 3-1 counts esp. go behind the mound—breathe—focus on task. "good low strike" etc. Another cue is when you get the sign, repeat pitch and location internally . . . e.g. "slider away" . . . repeat that in your mind . . . helps increase focus.

ANDREW: You nailed it. It's hard when the lineup is Mookie, Ortiz, Hanley, Bogey, etc. pre-pitching breathing will be a key for me to slow it down and have better self-talk.—Trust and believe.

TEWKS: Yes, I think you could have regrouped a tad better in some counts versus us . . . fuck the lineup! You're Andrew Miller!! Hitters don't want to face you! They are uncomfortable right from the beginning . . . take advantage of that. Increased focus on your controllables . . . .

ANDREW: Yeah—I wasn't as sharp as I need to be. I survived but could be better. Thanks for the refresher . . . haha.

TEWKS: Self-talk focused on what you want to do . . . delete negative talk by swiping the rubber, tapping your leg, whatever . . . then focus on task, with what u want to do. Great to chat. Best of luck.

ANDREW: Of course. Thanks again. Don't be a stranger, if I can ever help with anything don't hesitate. I run around telling everyone how important you were to me going to the Sox and how much I used you so I am at least good for that.

Just reaching out to say good job led to a "refresher" mental skills session, which occurred because of a couple of essential components necessary in any successful, long-term human interaction: trust and a solid relationship. And one thing this exchange illustrates is that even the most accomplished among us are not confident all of the time. Not that you could tell that from Andrew's *exterior*. Among the methods I've used when working with pitchers is the analogy of acting. When Tom Hanks or Denzel Washington is asked to star in a movie, what does he do? He transforms himself into that character. He role plays with words and actions (including body language) to make the person he is playing believable. I encourage pitchers to do the same when they take the field. Do they want to play the role of the timid, passive, afraid pitcher? Or do they want to play the role of the aggressive, confident, attacking pitcher?

Few players were more riveting that October than Miller, who became the poster boy in an emerging national conversation centered around how managers should deploy their most lethal bullpen weapons. After the Indians routed us, Miller went on to become the MVP of the AL Championship Series as he shut out a loaded Toronto lineup on three hits in 7.2 innings pitched while striking out fourteen and walking none. The eventual World Series champion needs eleven postseason wins—three in the Division Series, four in the League Championship Series and four more in the World Series. After our exchange, the only other texts I sent Miller that postseason were numbers counting down each win, and how many more until the title: 7 . . . 6 . . . 5 . . . 4 . . . and so on through Game 7 against the Cubs, down to 1, the number that never arrived for Miller and the Indians.

NOW, FROM MY PERCH on this mountaintop, cactus needles stinging and my wounded pride barking, my own countdown was on, big time. I continued my descent slowly, angling along the side of Camelback, on high alert for the cholla cacti, stopping to drink from my plastic water bottle as needed. I have no idea how long it took, but when I was finally, safely around that high ledge, I could see a way to forge a path that would land me safely on the fairway of the

Phoenician golf course some 150 yards below. Forget the "real" path at this point. I was headed straight down to the flat ground of the beautifully manicured golf course. And once I reached it, man, did that flat ground feel good.

Fairway clear, I walked across the plush, green grass to the cart path and headed back toward the entrance of the Cholla Trail a couple of hundred yards away. As I did, in full survival mode, I passed (and ignored) the posted signs: **NO WALKING OR BIKE RIDING ALLOWED ON PATH**. *Yeah, right*, I thought. *Somebody just try to stop me!* My just-out-of-the-box, shiny, brand-new Nike turf shoes were covered in even more desert dust than my ego. The skin on my right thigh and left ankle was swollen and punctured with hundreds of tiny holes. Maybe this wasn't the traditional exit off Camelback Mountain, but as I also tell the players I work with: "Each of us has our own path. There is a different route for everyone, and that's okay."

And, *phew*, talk about a different path. The past few months had taken me in directions I wouldn't have seen coming even a year before. Watching Miller, Rizzo, Jon Lester and Rich Hill work their magic in the postseason, and tracking many of the other players I've worked closely with as they've progressed . . . No, none of us ever know when the winds will change and our own personal GPS will reset. But you can take steps to ensure you're mentally prepared and in a place to succeed when it happens.

I made it back to my car, sat down and drew a long, deep breath. On the short drive back to my apartment, I stopped for some medical supplies: ice, Band-Aids, Neosporin and a six-pack of Bud Light. Like any grown man who just almost fell off a mountain, I gulped two beers and *then* treated my wounds. I sat there on the couch, another beer in hand, ice on my leg and so many thoughts and emotions jumping through my mind like, ahem, so many cholla needles. A part of me was beating myself up. *Do you know how stupid that was? You could have died!* Yet, another part of me was exhilarated. It was the closest I had ever been to death—at least, that's how I perceived it—and I felt really good that I had coached myself down the mountain. As the ice melted, the beer drained and it sank in that I had done it by using the same mental skills techniques I employed on the mound as a pitcher and now teach as a coach—*slow down, breathe, positive self-talk, focus on the task at hand*—it made me feel even better.

As we each find our own path to get to where we need to be in life, the journey can be made less harrowing by having reference points in place that we can gauge time and again. Touchstones that not only prevent us from becoming lost but, just as importantly, help keep nudging us forward in the process. I can tell you from experience, cacti aren't it.

On the other hand, now I know why they call it the Cactus League.

1

Breathe

Breathe. That is where this book begins, and it is where this book will end. Breathe. A concept so simple a newborn grasps it as soon as he greets the world. An act that eventually becomes so difficult an old man on his deathbed can no longer accomplish it.

In between, breath sustains life. And if you can master the art of controlling it, it can reduce blood pressure, improve sleep, maintain health, sharpen focus, improve job performance and, yes, in so many of our lives, cause stress to melt clear away like March ice on Opening Day.

Breathe. It is where we were midsummer in 2013, and Jon Lester had had it.

Around him, the Oakland Coliseum, a rapidly deteriorating ball-park that he detested, had never looked so untamable. Behind him, the first half of an inconsistently choppy season continued to clutter his mind. Ahead of him, the second half of a season that refused to produce answers appeared just as ominous.

At this point in its cracked-concrete life, the Coliseum was becoming notorious for sewage backups. Seriously. The major leagues? A plumbing system that may as well have been constructed during the California Gold Rush periodically caused toilets to back up, water to leak into both clubhouses and dugouts, and a resulting stench that could singe the hairs in your nostrils.

Breathe? Hold that thought. The Oakland Coliseum maybe isn't the best place in the major leagues to preach this concept. Yet there I was, in my role as a mental skills coach for the Boston Red Sox, late afternoon, sitting in the dugout anyway.

The periodic sewage, the stench, the antiquated clubhouses, none of that, by the way, is why Jon Lester disliked the place. What so many outside the game don't always understand is that every single road trip is foreign. Every field has a different look, a different view, a different background. Comfort breeds confidence, and nothing this side of health is more vital to a professional athlete than confidence.

Always, it seemed, for whatever reason, Lester was uncomfortable on the mound in the Oakland Coliseum. Every time he started a game there, the whole place just looked different.

"I don't know what it is," he says. "There are stadiums you get to and it never looks good. You always feel isolated. Detroit's one of those for me. You get on that mound and nothing looks right. It just doesn't fit you, for whatever reason. Toronto was the complete opposite. I love Toronto. I thought their mound was one of the best mounds in baseball. The way the backdrop is, it makes you feel like home plate is right there.

"Oakland was one of those places I never felt good in. I think it's because of the [massive] foul ground. Home plate, it looks like you're throwing to the batting cage over there. I've never really had good games there. So you have these different things that go through your mind when you get in these different places."

In the previous season, Lester had limited the Athletics to just one run and four hits over 6.2 innings, striking out nine and walking just one. But the Red Sox lost 3-2. Never had a good game in Oakland? As my old manager in Minnesota, Tom Kelly, often said, "The mind is a very dangerous thing."

On this day, there was a lot on Lester's mind, and too much of it was diminishing returns. At 8-5 with a 4.60 ERA, 2013 in so many ways was a continuation of 2012, statistically the worst of his career: 9-14 with a career-worst 4.82 ERA. For the man who worked five and two-thirds incredibly impressive shutout innings as a rookie in Game 4 of the 2007 World Series at Colorado's hitter-friendly Coors Field, this was foreign land, uncharted territory, a rock and a hard place he never would have imagined. Too many negatives were living rent free inside his head.

At twenty-nine and with the All-Star break waiting on the other side of the weekend, Lester was set to make his final start of the first half on Saturday night. At this point, he was certain of only one thing. What he was not going to do was step into the break without exhausting his search for solutions.

As David Ortiz, Dustin Pedroia, Jacoby Ellsbury and the rest of the Red Sox swung away in batting practice on this Friday afternoon, Lester looked into the dugout and spotted a potential life vest. He and I had first met in 2002, when Lester was eighteen, shortly after the Red Sox scooped him up in the second round of the draft. As part of my work with the Red Sox, I made it a point to meet as many minor-leaguers as I could as they entered Boston's system. Just as the ball is held together with those red stitches, so, too, are the relationships in this game. They can never be tight enough.

Even with Lester now pitching for the Chicago Cubs and me having moved on to become the mental skills coach of the San Francisco Giants, he continues to speak in fond terms of our times together.

"When you're in the minor leagues, anytime you can talk to someone who played in the majors, you feel like they're offering something," Lester says. "Tewks talked about different things as far as the mental side of the game, and building that relationship with him I had a trust where I could go and bounce things off of him. He's a no-BS guy. I knew he wouldn't pussyfoot around with me. I knew if I asked him a question, he would give me an honest answer, both on the pitching side and on the mental side. I knew I would get that from him."

I had come to this role, a Mr. Goodwrench for the mind, if you will, after thirteen years in the major leagues and a few more during which I obtained my master's degree in sports psychology and counseling from Boston University.

My first career, as I refer to it, includes one All-Star appearance, one third-place finish in National League Cy Young Award voting, 110 career wins and one of the lowest walk rates in baseball history. The radar gun did not dance and sing while this was happening. No, when I finally was able to outrun a series of false starts and one significant shoulder surgery, I did so by using my mind to impose my will. As John Tudor, one of my former teammates with the St. Louis Cardinals, once said, "Anyone can pitch with a 93 m.p.h. fastball. It takes courage to pitch throwing 84." Amen.

In my second career, the one I'm waist deep into and thoroughly enjoying now, I'm still trying to hit key spots with my mind. Only instead of specific locations on the plate—down and away, up and in—I work hard to pinpoint the spots that will help others thrive. Mental skills is an area of tremendous growth in this game right now. I'm proud to say I am one of the trailblazers.

I found out later that when the Red Sox were employing a full-court press to sign Lester as a free agent in the winter of 2014–2015, after I had left the Red Sox organization the first time to work for the Major League Baseball Players' Association, Boston officials made it a point to tell Lester during a recruiting trip to his Georgia home, before the news would become public, that they had reached an agreement to bring me back into the organization.

Maybe no small part of the reason they included me in their pitch to Lester was because of this cool day in the Bay Area that started with the big left-hander's approach and delivery.

Preparation never was a weakness for Lester. Few worked as hard as he did. But there was one area I felt could help improve his performance. I told him how I used mental imagery throughout my career. You've heard the expression "mental imagery"? The body doesn't know the difference between a real or an imagined event and, therefore, the body will go where the mind takes it. During the tough times, mental imagery exercises I had developed helped me battle the fear of failure and insecurity that, always, are an athlete's toughest opponent. During the good times, the mental imagery reinforced the foundation upon which I operated.

The short answer was that, no, Lester had never tried imagery before any of his starts. He had flirted with the idea of it just once, long ago, and he didn't like it for a very interesting reason.

Lester was never much of a reader because his admittedly short attention span just won't allow it, but he nevertheless devoured the legendary Harvey Dorfman's *The Mental ABC's of Pitching: A Handbook for Performance Enhancement* when he was in high school. He read it in three days, matter of fact. It was during his senior year, and he had decided to not play basketball that winter in order to focus on baseball, and he read the book about a week before his first start.

Looking for a way to focus amid the swirl of professional scouts and college recruiters who were creating chaos in his life at the time, Lester inhaled the book and immediately went out and threw a no-hitter in that first start, punching out nineteen hitters. He came within one out of a perfect game.

And that is why, more than a decade later, he still shied away from imagery. Because, as he told me, he just knew he could not replicate the success of that no-hitter with nineteen strikeouts.

"It just so happened that it was one of those days that just kind of fell in line with what I was doing and I was like, 'I can't get back to that place. If I try to do imagery again, it won't replicate the outcome,'" Jon says.

"That's the first thing you think of when you do it. You think of the last time you did it and what happened."

I shared my personal experiences of having used imagery for most of my career, and how powerful a mental tool it had been for me. He seemed intrigued. I asked if he would be willing to try a guided imagery exercise with me to give him a feel for what I was talking about. It was the right moment. At this point, Lester was open to anything that might help him.

We walked up the long tunnel leading from the dugout back into the visitors' clubhouse and disappeared into a small office. He sank into a leather couch. He slouched down, getting comfortable, his head leaned back against the top of the couch. In full Red Sox uniform, he tugged his baseball cap forward, tilted to shield his eyes from the room's harsh fluorescent light.

"Okay, now that you are comfortable, I want you to close your eyes and focus on your breathing," I told him.

I spoke slowly, softly. "Inhale through your nose . . . feel the air as it slowly passes down through the back of your throat and into your lungs ... feel your chest rise and expand ... now hold it ... now exhale slowly and fully through your mouth."

We repeated that sequence three times. As we did, I noticed Jon gradually sink deeper into the couch. His jaw loosened. His mouth opened slightly. His leg twitched. I paused, surprised he had become so relaxed so quickly.

"You are now relaxed and ready for your imagery practice," I said.

Following a few seconds of silence, I continued. "Now, imagine yourself on the pitcher's mound tomorrow night. Feel your spikes as they rest firmly on the pitching rubber. Feel the seams of the baseball as you grip the ball in your glove, which you hold up directly in front of you."

I led him through game situations. Through facing two batters while pitching from the windup. One batter while pitching from the stretch. I worked to create pictures in his mind, each associated with a particular pitch. Fastballs down and away for called strikes. Change-ups cloaked in the illusion of fastballs, creating swings and misses. Slow curveballs floating in for strikes, the hitters helplessly watching them go by. Deadly cutters that made those hitters look foolish.

I went through each batter he would see in Oakland's lineup the next night. I detailed various situations he might face and how he would successfully respond to them. Someone commits an error, this is how you react to it.

This imagery exercise went on for about eight minutes, and then I instructed Jon to open his eyes and reorient himself to the room. When he nudged his cap up off of his face, he looked like he had been sleeping. *Wow*, I thought. *He really got into this*.

"What did you think?" I asked. He said he liked it but that at times my dialogue went a little too fast. Because of that, at times, he said, he struggled to fully create images in his mind. This was good feedback for next time. Most important, there would be a next time. He was buying in.

We agreed to implement this brief imagery practice into his pre-game routine the next night. The best time, we decided, would be after his pitcher's meeting, around five o'clock. Before each start, the starting pitcher, catcher and pitching coach meet to go over that night's opposing lineup and implement a game plan. Right after that, Lester would go to the trainer's room, lie on the table, cover his eyes and re-create, as best he could, what we had just done.

On the field that Saturday night, Lester felt more comfortable than he had all season. He threw a called third strike by Coco Crisp to start the bottom of a 1-2-3 first inning. Induced a ground-ball double play in the second from Nate Freiman and wound up stranding two Athletics and holding them off the scoreboard. Derek Norris touched him for a solo homer in the fifth, and then Oakland scratched two more runs off of him in the sixth.

But on this night, the internal results following his session the night before became the most important element.

"It was almost like I had already pitched," Lester says. "I felt more relaxed and prepared. We lost 3-0, but I pitched a lot better. I felt more in command with what was going on in the game, with situations that arose during the game."

We talked again the next day about implementing imagery and visualization permanently into his pregame routine. We decided that I would record a guided imagery program for him to use prior to his starts during the season's second half. We discussed the content and timing of the script that day, and I made the recording during the All-Star break.

Over thirteen starts during the second half of the season, Lester would go 7-2 with a 2.57 ERA. Best of all, that run would stretch deep into October, where a quiet room in Fenway Park and an imagery program on Lester's iPod would combine to become as beautiful in Boston as the autumn orange- and red-tinged trees along the Charles River . . .

BREATHE. On a ninety-three-degree, mid-June night in St. Louis in 1990, I could have used a scenic and placid sight exactly like that. In fact, I really could have used someone like *me*.

At twenty-nine, with my major league career hanging precariously from a thread that seemed like it was twisting from the top of the Gateway Arch, the circumstances of my own career were so different from those of Lester at that age.

Back in those days, when grand old characters with names like Whitey Herzog, Sparky Anderson and Stump Merrill roamed the earth's dugouts, any player who requested a visit with a mental skills coach would have been plopped onto the first bus back to Toledo, or Springfield, or Oneonta, where I threw my first professional pitch in 1981.

They didn't have mental skills coaches.

They had men like Ted Simmons.

Don't get me wrong. I love Ted Simmons. I love him in no small part because he was the man who saved me from the discard pile. He fought for me to get a chance. Whatever we're doing in life, we all need people who have our back. You never forget the people who do.

Over the past year and a half at Triple-A Louisville, I had gone 16-7 with a 2.43 ERA. I had started the '90 season in the St. Louis bullpen, made eight appearances and then was optioned back to Louisville in early May. Then and the year before, every time the Cardinals dipped into their minor league system in need of a starting pitcher, it seemed like they were looking in every direction but mine. They plucked pitchers with better arms than mine, guys who threw harder, guys who were younger, guys who filled out every part of a scouting report you could imagine. Except me.

Life in the minor leagues, you get tired of it after a while. Especially when you've been drafted nine years earlier—thank you, New York Yankees—battled your way up the chain as a nineteenth-round pick and recently fought your way back from a shoulder surgery that left you wondering whether you'd suddenly have to begin the second chapter of your life far sooner than you were prepared for.

To that point in 1990, I had pitched in a grand total of forty-six big-league games for the New York Yankees, Chicago Cubs and St. Louis. Of those, thirty-four were starts. I was nowhere near as financially secure at twenty-nine as Lester was. Though he was still in the middle of a club-friendly deal, he had already earned roughly $20 million by then. On my end at that point, Laura and I had married less than two years earlier, in January 1989. She was still working as an assistant to the president of Concord Hospital. I was confident that my arm would bounce back. So we bought a very modest Cape Cod house, figuring it was something we could afford while we saw how things went.

Maybe we should have rented. The more the Cardinals bypassed me, the more frustrating it became. I began to look for an exit. Unable to get to Busch Stadium, I wanted to get far away from the bush leagues. How far? I even began talking about going to Japan to play.

Where Lester was frustrated with his own individual performance that day in Oakland because he knew he could pitch better at twenty-nine, I still didn't even know whether I could pitch in the big leagues at all. I was looking to secure both my own existence and a place in the game.

Then, the Cardinals called.

And when I arrived in St. Louis a day later with the promise of my first start in 1990, the farm director who helped pave the way cornered me against a concrete wall in the tunnel outside the Cardinals' clubhouse.

"You're going to get the ball on Saturday," Simmons told me. "And if you do well, you'll get it again. If not, I am not sure what will happen."

How's that for imagery? It scared the piss out of me. Yet, it's something every player wants to hear. *Just give me a chance. If I can't do it, I'll be the first one to go home.*

Simmons has been described by more than a few in the baseball world as "an acquired taste," and they—and I—mean that in the best possible way. He is a no-nonsense baseball savant. Doesn't suffer fools. Following a well-decorated, twenty-one-year career behind the plate with St. Louis, Milwaukee and Atlanta, he became a well-respected executive and scout.

Once you get past that sandpaper exterior coated with the dust of a few thousand infields, the knowledge and the stories flow from Simmons's worldly, razor-sharp mind. St. Louis picked him in the first round (tenth overall) of the 1967 draft out of the University of Michigan, back in the days of hippies and Vietnam. He went back to school during the off-seasons, and one icy winter weekend, Ted was hitchhiking home from Ann Arbor with his then girlfriend (now wife), Maryanne, when a van pulled over. After he helped Maryanne into the front seat, Simmons climbed into the back, where all the seats had been removed to make room for a full drum kit.

"Where ya going?" the driver asked.

"Detroit," Simmons replied.

That settled, Simmons noted that the driver must be a musician, introduced himself and Maryanne and inquired as to the driver's name.

"Bob Seger," came the reply.

A local legend who had yet to break nationally at the time, it would be only a few more years until *Live Bullet* and *Night Moves* rocketed Seger to stardom.

"He wasn't huge yet," Simmons says. "Then he got huge. It was just super of anybody to stop. He could have been a serial killer."

Now here we were, a decade after Simmons's one-time ride wrote the classic song, and I definitely was running against the wind.

"Bobby had pitched in Triple-A over the past two years and dominated," Simmons says. "Our manager at the time was Whitey Herzog, and Tewksbury was a finesse pitcher, to say the very least. Even though he had won all of those games in Louisville, it was very difficult for Mike Jorgensen, our Triple-A manager at the time, and myself to convince anybody that this guy should pitch because he was a slow, curveball, finesse pitcher. Not the most desirable to bring to the majors.

"After talking with Whitey and Dal Maxvill [St. Louis's general manager at the time], I was able to convince them to give him a chance. If he doesn't pitch well, we'll send him back. They finally said, 'Okay, bring him up here.' I knew both well enough to know that if Bob didn't pitch well, he wasn't coming back. I wanted to see and talk to him specifically, because I'm straightforward, no foolishness. 'Bob, here's the facts. I don't want you to be disillusioned or disappointed. You have to pitch well Saturday. If not, you're going back to the minors. You *have* to pitch well, and I've come to wish you all the luck.'"

Making the situation even more dire was this. When the Cardinals optioned me back to the minors five weeks earlier, I was out of options. Which meant they had to run me through waivers, meaning any other big-league club could claim me as its property and give me a uniform.

I desperately was hoping for this as an avenue back to the majors. Yet, all twenty-five other teams passed. So here I was, literally cornered between Simmons and a Busch Stadium concrete wall, my future after Saturday as murky as the Mississippi River a few blocks away.

Over those next few days, as I returned to the imagery practice that had been so powerful in New York when I was with the Yankees, jangled nerves gave way to a calmness. Even if it was for just one day, I again, finally, had some control over my situation.

Coming into the game, I knew the Montreal Expos were hot. They had won three in a row, five of six and eight of ten. I knew they neither struck out nor walked much. This team liked to swing the bat. I knew I was going to throw well that day. In a strange sort of way, everything was aligned. Just as certain ballpark settings can make you feel more or less comfortable, so, too, can certain opposing lineups. I knew many of the Expos players, having faced them in the minor leagues. And the imagery work left me feeling at peace.

With all due respect to Spike Owen, Tom Foley and Mike Fitzgerald, I felt like those guys weren't going to do damage off of me (although Fitzgerald did bang a fifth-inning triple to set up Montreal's first run). I was more worried about Tim Wallach and Andrés Galarraga. I wasn't even that worried about Tim Raines. I knew he was a great player, but I felt comfortable pitching against him. I knew I could throw him fastballs away, and because he dove over the plate so much, I felt I could get the ball in on him and minimize damage.

Davey Martinez, Montreal's leadoff hitter, was a teammate of mine with the Cubs in 1987 and 1988. I knew he had a tough combination of power and speed and didn't strike out often. But I had more difficulty with contact hitters, and these Expos were a free-swinging team. As I worked on my imagery, that, too, added to my confidence. My entire approach was to put the ball in play while taking the sting out of their bats.

So despite the pressure, uncertain future, a skeptical manager in my dugout and 43,553 in the stands, the mound became a very peaceful place. I struck out Martinez to start the game, gave up a two-out double to Raines in the first but then got Galarraga to ground to third.

Second inning went 1-2-3 on just seven pitches, then I worked around a one-out double from pitcher Kevin Gross to finish a scoreless third and then went 1-2-3 in the fourth. It was 0-0 and my confidence was rock solid.

We had a chance to score in the fourth when Ozzie Smith and Willie McGee rapped base hits to start the inning, and I was thinking it sure would be great to get a lead, but they were stranded.

By the fifth, I began to feel a little pressure in my performance, and when Fitzgerald punched a one-out line drive to right field for a triple, the heat on this ninety-three-degree day shot up immediately. Foley singled him home and, after another out, my old buddy Martinez cracked a two-run homer to put Montreal up 3-0.

In my mind, there was no time to fret. We scored two runs in the bottom of the fifth, and I knew I had to recover and pitch a couple of more innings to make this a good outing and continue to give my team a chance to win. Facing the heart of the Montreal lineup in the sixth, I induced a ground ball from Raines and then got consecutive fly balls from Galarraga and Wallach.

After Milt Thompson's RBI single evened the game at 3-3 in the bottom of the sixth, I kept the Expos off the board in the seventh. That was it for my day. Seven innings, three runs, eighty pitches, sixty-one strikes and, given that we came back to win 5-3, a 1-0 record. I left with a good feeling, like, whew, okay, I cleared one hurdle. I felt like I was going to get the ball again, maybe the performance against the Expos would even earn me at least a couple of more starts.

I don't remember a lot in the immediate aftermath of that start, but a week later in Chicago against my old Cubs, I got the ball again—and earned another victory. What happened after that Expos game was my old pitching coach, Mike Roarke, asked what day did I want to throw on the side? I always liked my bullpen day to be on the third day after I started instead of on the second day after.

Roarke didn't say a whole lot and, when he did, he mumbled. There wasn't a lot of communication in those days. You did a lot of waiting, wondering and tea-leaf reading.

What I didn't need communicated, however, was this. Hitters don't like to hit from behind in the count, even against soft throwers. I used this to my advantage while mentally cat-burgling my way through the game for the next nine years, and this was as important to my imagery and visualization preparation as Galarraga's bat was to his impressive career.

That day was like starting all over again. A kind of rebirth, with some sharpened skills that would not only help me then, but allow me to help others, like Lester, a generation or two down the line, as baseball became more and more enlightened where the mental game was concerned.

When I see Simmons today, he always gives me a big smile, like, "I remember that talk." It's one of those things, I think, where as an instructor or coach, when you have faith in a player and the player comes through, you feel happy you fought for the player.

I remained in the Cardinals' rotation the rest of that season (going 10-9 with a 3.23 ERA in twenty starts), through Herzog's firing and Joe Torre's hiring, and for four more seasons after that. Then I signed free-agent contracts with Texas, San Diego and Minnesota, continuing to visualize my way through moments both big and small, mind-crafting my way through fearsome opposing lineups with low radar-gun readings but deft command of my fastball.

Some games, things went close to the mental script I had laid out beforehand. Others didn't. But I had my foundation, my anchor, and that prepared me for everything. And anything.

One day in 1995 when I was with the Rangers, I returned to pitch in Fenway Park, just seventy miles from my home. We won a wild one, 9-8, scoring eight earned runs against Roger Clemens in the first four innings. I only lasted four and two-thirds innings myself, giving up six hits and six runs. And as I walked to my car afterward, wouldn't you know it, I saw an SUV stopped in the street near the players' parking lot, mobbed by fans. The parking lot attendant informed me it was Clemens.

So I threaded my way through, approached the vehicle from the passenger side, opened the door and hopped in, figuring I would commiserate with him. In one hand, I was carrying a bouquet of flowers a fan had given me. In the other, I was carrying a paper sack containing a few beers.

Thinking it was a fan entering his SUV, Clemens wheeled around, fist cocked. I thought he was going to belt me.

"What the hell?!"

"Hey, Roger, it's Tewks! You should lock the doors, you dumbass—anybody could come in here!"

We laughed hard about that the next day, imagining the Boston newspaper headlines reporting the Rocket actually swung and clobbered me: *Clemens, Tewksbury Square Off after Poor Outings*.

Point is, some nights in the big leagues, flowers work. Others, you need beer. Whether you're Jon Lester, Roger Clemens or me.

But *always*, you need to slow down and breathe.

2

A Salesman
on the Mound

"Baseball is 90 percent mental. The other half is physical." That's what Yogi Berra said, mathematics and fractions be damned. Like Yogi might say, I was always interested in the mental side of the game before I knew I was interested in the mental side of the game.

You know those dreams where you're running and running and running and no matter how fast or how far you run, you still cannot catch up to your target? Well, long ago, there was a bus. It was a team bus. The team bus of the Rutgers University Scarlet Knights baseball squad, and it was traveling toward a game.

Except, this wasn't a dream. This was real life. And the issue was very, very real. I was a lost soul at the time, overwhelmed by the big university, head spinning from city life, a small-town kid trying on a pair of shoes six sizes too big. There were more people in my dormitory at Rutgers than there were in my entire hometown of Salisbury, New Hampshire. So as that bus rolled down the street past the post office, a bus I was supposed to be riding, I happened to emerge on foot from the post office at *the exact same time*. Talk about your wrong addresses.

Some of my teammates recognized me, the bus pulled over and from inside came the order from longtime coach Matt Bolger: "Get on the bus!" All of the players were dressed in uniform, prepared for the long, cold day at Seton Hall. Me? I was just walking from my dorm to the post office and back. I certainly wasn't dressed for my punishment for mixing up my schedule and briefly going AWOL: shouldering the day's grunt work by charting pitches for both ends of the doubleheader, from a perch on the cold metal bleachers. Looking back now from a few decades down the road, maybe I could read deep into this moment and philosophize about how in my second career, this incident helped me to identify others following their own path, allowing me to connect with guys like Lester, and Anthony Rizzo, and Andrew Miller, who would help pitch the Cleveland Indians into the 2016 World Series against the Chicago Cubs.

Or, maybe before you can help others, you simply must find yourself.

I had some searching to do in those early years.

I had landed at Rutgers because my high school principal, Bob Norton, played football and baseball there. He knew Bolger, helped get me some financial aid and, boom, I was in. Plus, in all of my small-town naïveté, I thought being in proximity to New York City would be a good thing for what I hoped would be my life's work in baseball. As a proud son of New England, I well remembered the epic, one-game, sudden-death playoff between the New York Yankees and Boston Red Sox in 1978 that sent the Yankees toward a second consecutive World Series title over the Los Angeles Dodgers. Bucky Bleeping Dent, indeed. Boston loses, *and* I wind up over my skis at Rutgers.

Like so many other kids, I loved baseball from an early age. I grew up in a small apartment a block away from White Park in Concord, New Hampshire, an idyllic place offering the lure of baseball and softball fields, tennis courts, a pond and a swimming pool. One spring day when I was seven, I went wandering around the park, encountered a group of adults conducting sign-ups for the upcoming season and, well, with my mom and dad not with me, I signed myself up. A couple of days later there was a ringing telephone, a coach, a first practice, uniform No. 7 and, because of my strong arm, the third-base job for the Concord Group Insurance team. I was on my way.

Later that summer, we moved to a small town called Salisbury, thirty minutes north of Concord, and only the location changed. My love for the game did not. All I wanted to do back then was play baseball, and each spring I couldn't wait to get outside and get going. In those days, I dragged my brother Keith, who is one year younger than me, outdoors for games of catch but would become frustrated with his inability to accurately throw the ball back to me. So when that happened, I would throw the ball back to Keith harder, and then harder, and then . . . of course, the result was he would quite often miss it and the ball would land in a distant snowbank or get stuck in the mud. And, of course, good old Keith would retrieve the ball and then intentionally throw it over my head, bringing a quick end to our game of catch. Ah, brothers.

Frustrated by these frequent disagreements, early in my high school years I would eventually walk up the street to a nearby elementary school packing a piece of chalk, a couple of old, scuffed-up baseballs, my glove and a vivid imagination. With the chalk, I would draw a strike zone on the school wall. With my feet, I would mark off sixty feet, six inches. With my mind, I would create a pretend, opposing lineup. Then, I would pitch. Unlike my brother, the wall always threw it back and was never a no-show.

Through plenty of trial and no small amount of error, and not that I realized this at the time, I was figuring out that so many limitations are self-constructed. Even though we may not see them as quickly as we would like, there are different paths leading around so many obstacles. We just need to find them.

It was during the summer before my senior year of high school when I collected some two-by-fours and some chicken wire and erected a crude, personal version of the popular pitchbacks that soon would be sold at a sporting goods store near you. Perfect (except for the part that I wasn't exactly worldly enough to patent the darned thing). Now, I needed neither Keith nor any other battery mate. I could pitch and fine-tune my command on my own, spend all kinds of hours practicing my craft, home in on areas I hoped would take me deep into the baseball world even after my high school career was finished.

Obsessed, self-absorbed and often impatient—yep, three of the classic characteristics of a teenage boy—my brother Shawn, five or six at the time, one day accompanied me and kept drifting behind the screen. I warned him several times to move out of the way. Then he moved in too close one too many times, and what I viewed as my impeccable control suddenly abandoned me. Next thing I knew, I had drilled him right between the eyes, Shawn went down in a heap, blood pooled everywhere and I frantically carried him back into the house explaining to my mother what had happened. My parents rushed him to the hospital, twenty minutes away, and I sat home fighting to keep the demons at bay. I was sick over Shawn's injury. Upset with myself for not being more patient. Guilt ridden about what this mishap would do to my parents financially, since they scraped to make ends meet, lived paycheck to paycheck, and I was sure they had no insurance.

Crazy, the moments and thoughts that stick with you from all those years ago. But they all flow into making us who we are today, building our character, shaping our thinking and, if we're lucky, forging some of the mental tools that afford us the opportunity to fix things several miles on up the road when life periodically forces us to pull off to the shoulder, engine smoking. Had you told Shawn that night that I would go on to pitch for thirteen seasons in the major leagues with a walks-per-nine-innings rate of 1.45, no. 1 on baseball's all-time list of starting pitchers since the dead-ball era (minimum 1,500 innings), I'm quite sure he would have taken issue with that.

Truth is, still awkward and lacking confidence, I wouldn't have believed it, either.

Control wasn't my forte, at least, not in the very beginning in so much of my life at the time. Deep within my love for the game was this simple fact: Baseball, for me, was an escape. My father was an auto mechanic, my mother mostly worked in child care in our home, and among myself, Keith (one year younger than me), our sister Roxanne (three years younger) and Shawn (twelve years younger), there was constant tension in the house brought on by financial instability and marital infidelity. As the oldest, I was all too aware of our financial burdens. And neither of my parents was faithful. They did the best they could, but they were married young (my father, Ken, was nineteen, and my mother, Shirley, was eighteen) and spent much time and significant energy playing from behind. It was a feeling I never wanted to experience myself.

My father never saw me play baseball when I was young. As a matter of fact, he never saw me pitch a major league game, either. He always said he never went to my games because he thought I wouldn't pitch well if he was there, like he was bad luck or something. Nevertheless, I left him tickets at Yankee Stadium one game during my rookie year, threw a complete game against the Tigers, and was so happy because I had proven his theory wrong. Afterward, I went out to the ticket office, our predetermined postgame meeting place, and . . . he wasn't there. I found out he never was there. The tickets were never picked up.

There was just a distance, and other priorities. Like survival. During the winter, on many nights he would return home, from "twisting wrenches" in various Concord garages, to frozen pipes in our double-wide trailer. The trailer sat on top of a hill and we had picturesque views of Mount Kearsarge to the north. It was the only good thing about the place. He would scoop up his torch, climb under the trailer or into the four-by-four cinder-block bunker that housed our water heater, aim the fire and warm up the pipes. Whether the pipes unfroze from the heat of the fire or that of his cursing, we probably needed a licensed plumber to authoritatively rule on that.

Eventually, as we lost our home to bankruptcy, it was real easy to limp toward the default position of "things just don't work out." It is a dangerous, toxic frame of mind that I, for one, would have to work extremely hard at changing as I grew into adulthood and did what I could to keep fueling the pilot light on my sometimes flickering dream.

So, escape. And as I grew older, no matter how sideways or upside down things got, always, there was one sure way to avoid the emotion and pain that life wrought: Go play. Go throw. Go run. My search was on. I was driven and I was creative, open to all options. I started using imagery and keeping a journal in high school. Though I for some reason got away from that in college, it became a part of the foundation I would return to, one that eventually would serve me exceptionally well.

But first, I had some navigating to do. At Merrimack Valley High School in Penacook, New Hampshire, we lost the Class I state title game my junior season 3-2 on a squeeze bunt. Then, my senior year, we were favored to win it all but were upset in the first round of the state tournament. We led 1-0 into the top of the seventh inning and I was three outs away from a perfect game ... and both were lost. I was crushed. Things just don't work out ... *noooo!*

Undrafted out of high school, the Boston Red Sox offered me a chance to sign as a free agent via scout Bill Enos that summer, and even though our family could have used the $14,000 offer (plus another $7,500 in incentives), close friends—Norton, the high school principal, and Dave Anderson, my high school coach—advised college instead. It would give me something to fall back on if pro ball didn't work out down the line, plus, my scholarship was valued at around $30,000. (Incidentally, as the proud dad of two recent college grads, how I wish that was the tuition amount now!)

Rutgers, here I came.

And there went the bus.

I was so homesick. I was so overwhelmed. The demands of college, both academically and socially, were like nothing I had ever encountered. On one of my first days on campus, I left my dorm room door unlocked while I went to the bathroom, and somebody waltzed right in and stole my roommate's wallet. Back home in small-town New Hampshire, we didn't even lock our doors, period. What was this? I didn't even make it a semester. Forget about wrong addresses. That day I was departing the post office as the bus rolled on by? You could have just stamped me "return to sender" right then and there. I was done.

So I went home and moved back in with my mother and younger brother, who, after my parents' divorce, were living in a two-bedroom apartment in Penacook, New Hampshire, across the street from a leather tannery not far from my high school. Not exactly the horsehide type of leather that till then had been the focal point of my life, I can tell you that. Pending wind direction, the smell sometimes was nearly unbearable. And I landed a job that fall at a mail-order bird-seed store. Fowl ball? Yeah, sure . . . but also a life lesson that sometimes the most pivotal moments on an individual journey can emerge during the most unlikely of times.

My gig at Duncraft, founded in 1952 and "America's number one resource for wild bird supplies," involved, among other things, filling orders and preparing them to be shipped. At the side of one upstairs room was a door that opened, with a ramp we would slide the orders down and onto a truck, which we pulled up to load on the one-way street down below. One late-fall day, I was lifting a box to plop onto the ramp when I happened to look through the door, and down below I spied a familiar face. It was Dave Anderson, my high school coach, advisor to go to college, close friend, father figure and a man I respected immensely. It was as if we were frozen in time. That moment, that one glimpse of him, seemed to go on forever.

Looking back through the decades today, I still really don't understand how or why he happened to be in that spot at that moment. That little one-way street was out of the way, bisecting two bigger streets, Main and Russell. When I glimpsed Dave, he was behind the truck we were loading, waiting to pass by. I was looking down at him, and he was looking up. Then he was gone. It wasn't like we exchanged hellos. There were no gestures. And yet, in that moment, the message I took away could not have been more clear. *Get out of Penacook! Now!*

Sure, maybe former New York Yankees pitcher Red Rolfe was a Penacook native. And Joe Lefebvre, the Yankees' third-round draft pick in 1977. Lefebvre homered against Toronto's Dave Stieb in his first big-league game and, later, batted cleanup for the Philadelphia Phillies in the 1983 World Series. So even though I played my high school games at Rolfe Park, it was Lefebvre to whom I hitched my mental wagon. *If he made it,* I thought, *so can I!* However, given my own personal and current longitude and latitude looking down at my old high school coach and mentor, surrounded by bird seed, this place did not exactly seem the best route to Yankee Stadium.

What was clear was that I needed an escape route out of Penacook, and I found one in the sunshine of Florida, at Saint Leo College, thirty-five miles north of Tampa. Saint Leo played baseball in the very good Division II Sunshine State Conference, and I was familiar with it because as a high school senior, I had visited Eckerd College in St. Petersburg, which had developed major-leaguers like Lefebvre and Steve Balboni, another major leaguer from New Hampshire. I entered Saint Leo as a redshirt freshman in January 1979, starting on the junior varsity team because I had to sit out a year as a transfer athlete. One of the assistant coaches at the time was a man who a few years earlier had been my coach in New Hampshire on the American Legion Post 21 team, Brian Sabean. He would soon would become the director of scouting, and then the vice president of player development and scouting for the New York Yankees, before moving on to become general manager and then president of baseball operations of the three-time World Series champions, the San Francisco Giants. It would not be the last time I would connect with him.

"You know what's funny—the way he pitched somewhat mirrored his artistic side," Sabean says about me today. "He's a pretty accomplished artist. He was a guy who had impeccable control, walked virtually nobody, always pitched to contact. He was cerebral and had that artistic side of him. It's not that long ago, but a lot of athletes don't want the outside world or even their teammates to know what their hobbies or distractions are. I'm not surprised Tewks's career has taken that path toward mental skills coaching."

It's true, I do draw. I do paint. It started at Merrimack Valley High School where my art teacher, Robin Denham, was fantastic. No matter what level of artist you were, Robin made you feel like the next Picasso. Her husband, Jim, was another of my high school mentors.

We used to play one-on-one basketball games during breaks in the school day for Nutty Buddies, those old, delicious ice cream cones. Sadly, Jim died at a young age. I still miss him.

Probably, it was my father who first led me down the artistic path. He was a doodler, and I remember him drawing cars and soldiers with the flair of a skilled cartoonist. Often, in the majors, I painted in my hotel room on the days I was to start. I've always enjoyed it. Athletes need a positive distraction, something that allows them to feel good about themselves that is unrelated to the result of a baseball game. Art was that for me. It is a relaxing outlet to release some of the internal pressure that builds up. And boy, for all of us, those internal pressures have a way of taking on a life of their own so quickly. Positive distractions are essential.

So, pay dirt at Saint Leo's? Well yeah, if I took the long view. Let's just say, in the very beginning, it was another good training ground that helped steel my mental game. We called ourselves the Killer B's on the junior varsity team, had a lot of fun and played a pretty good schedule. Then there was the day we piled into vans, drove the ninety minutes to the Manatee Junior College in Bradenton, Florida, I pitched and . . . was scorched for twenty runs in three innings. Yes, count 'em: twenty. All I remember from that day is line drives and baserunners, both all over the place. When I run across old Saint Leo teammates now, they still say balls were hit so hard that day that our guys in the field were diving out of the way for personal safety. Twenty runs allowed! And one other thing. I was replaced on the mound midgame by a theater major. Yes, a theater major.

You know the old Hallmark card bromide, that which does not kill you makes you stronger? Let me tell you, in baseball terms, being sent to the showers for a theater major who was just playing ball for something to do is Exhibit A in that department. Me? I got stronger, quick. Desperate times call for desperate measures, or something like that. Though I still flash back to that game every single time I am in Florida and traveling on I-75 past the Manatee Junior College sign, I survived. Now, I can smile, and even laugh. And when a young member of the San Francisco Giants organization or any other player today approaches with a significant psychological hurdle he needs to clear, among the many reference points I have to offer is this one. A theater major. *Hmfph!*

Things improved. I was invited to participate in the prestigious Cape Cod Baseball League in 1979. I played for the Wareham Gatemen and was a teammate and roommate of Rob Murphy, who would later pitch for Boston and Cincinnati. Today, most players in the Cape league live with host families. We didn't, and good thing, too. Nobody would have wanted us! There were five of us all living in a small, three-bedroom cottage about two miles from the field. We all had summer jobs, and we had a blast. One player worked at Cumberland Farms and quit after a week. On his last day of work, he made off with a few dozen eggs from a recently delivered order. Murphy's job was to shuttle the roommates back and forth to work, and the now ex–Cumberland Farms ballplayer decided to test his throwing accuracy by seeing how many mailboxes he could egg on the route back to our cottage, and, well, why stop there? Food fight! Bluto, Otter, D-Day and the rest of the gang from that smash-hit movie of the time, *National Lampoon's Animal House,* had nothing on us as we unloaded Cumberland Farms's haul all around an ill teammate, Freddie, as he was lying in bed in our screened-in porch, covering his head with a pillow and waiting for the eggs to run out (or, for us to grow up).

We really didn't know if Freddie was sick, had food poisoning or was just hungover. We never knew with Freddie. Once, he returned from a night of partying with singed eyebrows as a result of flaming shots gone bad. Now, all we knew was we had a big supply of eggs and everyone was fair game. As Bluto asked and answered during his rousing pep talk in the Faber College fraternity house: "Was it over when the Germans bombed Pearl Harbor? Hell, no!" And it was only just beginning for me, too.

A year later I was invited to another prestigious summer league, this one in Alaska. Alaskan summer league rosters consisted primarily of college stars from West Coast schools. I had a host family, a supermarket job and the challenge of becoming accustomed to the summer sun not setting. It was daylight most of the time. But more difficult than that was the fact that I couldn't pitch. I was there two weeks before being sent home with a sore shoulder. So it was back to Saint Leo, and then it turned out that, just like Red Rolfe had proved way back in 1931 and Joe Lefebvre in 1977, there really was a path that could lead from Penacook, New Hampshire, to Yankee Stadium. The Yankees picked me in the nineteenth round of the 1981 amateur draft, leading me to rookie-level ball in the wonderful small town of Oneonta, New York. My signing bonus was $5,000 plus what was called an "incentive" bonus, a cash bonus paid to players as they advanced through each level of the minors. The catch was you had to be with a team for ninety days before getting your bonus. Needless to say, in the summer of my rookie year, the $5,000 part of the bonus payment was a great gift.

Over the next four summers, rung by rung, I slowly climbed the ladder that was the Yankees' minor league system. Fort Lauderdale ... Nashville ... Albany ... Columbus. Minor league baseball quickly brings to life the words on the lyrics sheet from the Johnny Cash song of the same name: "I've been everywhere, man." And those times, they were quite different. In my first full professional season, at Fort Lauderdale in 1982, I went 15-4 with a 1.88 ERA in twenty-four games (23 starts). But the key numbers were these: at twenty-one years old, having barely broken the seal of pro ball, I threw thirteen complete games and 182.1 innings. Forget dog years. In today's manic pitch-count world, that's about three seasons in one for a still-learning minor-leaguer.

I paid. Going for my sixteenth win late in the season, I threw a pitch and felt a sharp pain in my elbow. I tried to throw one more pitch, hoping the pain would disappear, but my fingers were numb. Three months later, I underwent surgery at New York University Medical Center to move my ulnar nerve out of its natural spot in the elbow, where it was getting pinched, to another position on the inside of the elbow. The surgery worked well, but I lost some velocity in the process. My fastball slowed from an average of about 88 m.p.h. to the 84–85 range.

Still, the Yankees organization was fabulous to play for then, and it remains so today—especially for a minor-leaguer. You feel like you are in the lap of luxury. You are treated first class all the way. In those days, the Yankees always had more coaches per team than any other organization in baseball. More coaches, more reps, better players. One of our mantras back then, "If you can make it here, you can make it anywhere," was straight from Sinatra. We all felt that if we could get to Triple-A with the Yankees, we could play on any team in the majors. And by the next season, I was healthy and back on my way at Double-A Nashville. The driver who kept me and the others moving along on our way was a man named Snuffy, a part-time music producer and full-time bus driver. Where else but in Nashville, and minor league baseball, could you encounter such an invention? I loved to sit up on the front step of the bus next to Snuffy, talking baseball, life, and listening to music (Dan Fogelberg's "Run for the Roses" was our favorite song), especially in the early morning hours when the guys were asleep behind us. Sometimes, we would ride in silence while I just sat and watched the mile markers speed by. And in a wide-ranging league that included Knoxville, Memphis, Chattanooga, Orlando and Jacksonville, the mile markers were exhausting.

The long bus rides at times were rolling educational clinics:

- There were the negotiations regarding who sat where on the long trips, often dictated by the card players (four seats close to each other were needed) and Double-A veterans (who were afforded single seats to stretch out).
- There was literature *and* theater. The occasional, dramatic reading aloud by one of my teammates from the *Penthouse Forum*, extremely offensive to some and hysterically funny to others, plus material from upcoming comedian Andrew Dice Clay.
- There was debating. Once, our Hall of Fame pitching coach Hoyt Wilhelm caught wind that a lefty pitcher who was not starting the next night had snuck into the top bunk reserved for the next game's starter so he could lie down and sleep, so Hoyt angrily approached the bunk, pulled the pitcher down onto the floor and words were exchanged. I can still hear Hoyt, in his southern drawl: "Goddammit, King, get your ass out of that bunk!"
- There was biology. Matt Keough, a real, live major-leaguer, was sent to Nashville to learn the knuckleball from Wilhelm, a master, and we all felt like we were in the presence of royalty. I mean, we all knew who this guy was. He was what we wanted to be. His presence helped us all realize that the big leagues might be closer than we thought. But that didn't stop some of the guys from practicing the fine art of "pennying"—blocking the bathroom door in the bus from the outside by wedging pennies underneath it—one day when Keough stepped in to do his business. When Keough realized he was blocked, and not in the true biological sense, he started kicking at the door until one kick too many sent him recoiling into the back wall, causing him to smash the back of his head on the window and

begin bleeding as if in a scene from a television show. I can still remember his primal scream: "Get me the fuck out of here NOW!"

- And there was introduction to pharmacology. For the ride from Nashville to Orlando, more than ten hours long, veteran players not only brought the usual assortment of pillows, headphones and cassette tapes, but some also made sure to pack beer and NyQuil. One veteran pitcher had it all planned out. He was going to drain a few beers to start the trip, then suck down some NyQuil to ensure he slept for most of the ride.

Merrimack Valley, Rutgers and Saint Leo's might have been in my rearview mirror, but my education was continuing. I was amazed someone would do that. Looking back now, I can see that this veteran probably was depressed. He was somewhere around twenty-eight and stuck at Double-A. At some point comes the realization that a person is going to fall short of attaining his dream, and as far as we've come today, I am surprised more players are not speaking up about depression. It is real, and it is endemic, no matter what we do to attempt to disguise it. This is something I think athletes at all levels feel when their career is over, or ending. You lose an enormous part of who you are.

Then, like now, the minor league seasons did not last twelve months. In between, there was this thing called winter. A time to rest, a time to shiver, a time to find a job to help make ends meet. And if you played it right, also a time of continuing education.

Back home in Concord, New Hampshire, I obtained an off-season job at Mickey Finn's, an old-style sporting goods store where we sold just about everything: guns, ammo, Levi's, fishing equipment, shoes, sweaters, you name it. It was a great winter job with a lot of fun people, men and women. The days flew by during the Christmas shopping seasons, especially. By the end of those, we were all gassed. One

Christmas Eve, we locked the doors at closing time, 7 **P.M.** sharp, and then I did what any good, hard-working retail employee would do. I cracked a can of beer to celebrate. So, too, did several of my fellow employees.

About three minutes after we locked the front door, a man came knocking, begging to get in. I walked to the door and pointed to my watch, indicating that, sorry, buddy, we're closed. Too late. Then, for some reason, I reached back for just a little extra. I undid my belt buckle, turned and gave the man a close-up view of the full moon. The Budweiser? The end of a long day? What could be the cause of such outrageous behavior? Probably, just me and my sometimes quirky sense of humor.

Being that so much of this life, like baseball, is all about timing, I can only say thank goodness that man was not the older, well-dressed gentleman who stopped in one other Christmas shopping season with a young girl, maybe eight or nine, fortunately, this time during store hours. You never know when a person is going to step into your life and expand your mind, broaden your horizons, push your boundaries. For me, this was one of those moments.

There was an aura about this man, a calming manner that some-how felt different from all of the other men and women to whom I had sold shoes. My innermost instincts poked at my curiosity and, after a few moments, I asked him what he did for a living.

"I'm an author," he said.

"Oh, what kind of books do you write?" I asked.

"Mostly inspirational."

Now, he had me. When I told him I had read a lot of Norman Vincent Peale's work on the power of positive thinking, he responded that he was "good friends with Norman."

"Really? What is your name?"

"Og Mandino."

I had never bloody heard of him. So, I thought, he couldn't be much of a writer. Certainly not if his name didn't ring a bell with *me*. As if I had this vast reservoir of knowledge of the history of famous authors.

"That's great," I replied. "I'll have to look you up."

There was a bookstore down the street from Mickey Finn's so, after I clocked out that day, I wandered down to look up this guy Og Mandino. As I searched through the inspirational section, I was absolutely stunned to learn that I had just sold a pair of shoes to the author of the best-selling book *The Greatest Salesman in the World*.

In no time, I devoured Mandino's books and, on the heels of those, I tore through the books of Norman Vincent Peale, the seeds of my interest in psychology quickly and firmly beginning to take root. "I will act now," Mandino wrote while delivering a primary message of "Do it now." Repetitive actions build good habits. This made sense to me.

My mind was active. It was hungry. The more I read and thought, the more insatiable my mental appetite became. For me, a lot of this stuff was fertile territory. More than that, when the winters ended and new seasons started with those magical, sunblock-drenched words "pitchers and catchers report," I brought along my growing wealth of knowledge as part of my overall repertoire.

Outside the bus windows, the minor league towns passed by. By 1985, at twenty-four, my career felt like it was stalling. My fastball velocity was down thanks to the ulnar nerve surgery. I pitched at Double-A Albany-Colonie, went 6-5 with a 3.54 ERA in seventeen starts and felt completely at the mercy of whatever baseball forces were out there. Sometimes, it felt like they were beginning to conspire against me. Mostly, I suffered alone because there were no mental skills coaches back in the day, I was still figuring things out, didn't really have anybody with whom to share my thoughts and, besides, was unsure if I wanted to share anything with anybody anyway.

Years later, when I was a mental skills coach with the Red Sox, I met Dr. Steve Durant, a psychologist with Massachusetts General Hospital and a third-generation rugby player. I still remember the first time he spoke to Red Sox minor-leaguers one spring training. Two of the things he said stand out to me today, and I still use them in my own application. Do not suffer alone, and have a "go-to man," someone you can really count on, when things start to go sideways. Too many players still suffer alone or attempt to replace that loneliness with substances (booze or worse) or people who lead them in negative directions.

When I finally was promoted to Triple-A Columbus, Ohio, following two and a half seasons in Double-A, feeling like it was overdue, I walked into a bookstore while killing time before a game in a local mall. An audio book in the self-help section on improving performance caught my eye, and I purchased it. Always, in the down moments, something consistently led me into those self-help sections. I had a strong, natural interest in the subject but, really, no resources for learning.

When I popped the cassette into the player, Side 1 contained a breathing exercise, followed by a series of affirmations. Side 2 contained the same affirmations, but presented in a subliminal manner. Hmmm. I liked it. I felt a connection. So I incorporated listening to this tape into my daily routine. Every day, at the same time, in the locker room, I would lie on the floor with my feet up in my locker, a towel over my head and headphones over my ears.

Three decades later, I believe today what I began to believe while listening to that tape on all of those minor league locker-room floors. That my improved performance on the field that month happened from the inside out. That change—real, productive change—occurs in a person from the inside out.

My search was not yet finished, nor anywhere close to being finished. But I was thousands of miles past the point where, overwhelmed, confused and doubting, I missed that bus at Rutgers University. That audio program was the impetus not only for my improved performance that helped pull me out of neutral and put me back in the fast lane that season, but it also remains the catalyst for the audio programs I create for players in my current role as a mental skills coach. I really felt like I programmed my mind for success by listening to this audio recording as much as I did.

No longer did it feel like I was trying on shoes that were six sizes too big. Things were beginning to fit much better. As I did my running in those Triple-A outfields, I continually listened to Phil Collins sing "In the Air Tonight." When that 1985 season ended, I felt locked in both mentally and physically. That winter, I would lie in bed on those cold nights and keep listening: "I've been waiting for this moment all my life, hold on ... I've been waiting for this moment, all my life." Then that big, booming drum solo would send chills through my body.

Slowly, this dream I'd had, the imagery I was starting to focus on, was becoming a reality.

3

The Art of the Pitch

A day before the first major league spring training start of my career, I was picking up baseballs during batting practice in Florida alongside the great Catfish Hunter, who was in camp as an alumni coach and whose glittering career would land him the next summer in Cooperstown. Aside from having a great nickname, Catfish was a control artist who commanded home plate as well as his favorite fishing holes.

Always on the lookout for a learning opportunity and with deep admiration for Hunter, I figured this was a no-brainer. So I asked him, "Catfish, do you have any words of advice for a young pitcher trying to make a major league team?"

I can still see this picture today. Wearing his Yankees pullover sweatshirt, and with the omnipresent wad of chaw in his left cheek, Catfish casually turned his head toward me, spit out a thick, long stream of tobacco juice and said in that slow, North Carolina drawl: "Just throw strikes, kid. Throw strikes." *Splat!*

So much for the deep, dark mysteries of the big-league universe. Throw strikes? I could do that. I *had* to do that. I wasn't Nolan Ryan. Especially after my shoulder surgery in 1988, I didn't have the kind of fastball that would strike fear into the hearts of hitters. Truth be told, I didn't have the kind of fastball that would even jangle their nerves. Just listen to Fred McGriff, the "Crime Dog" himself, the slugger who pummeled 493 career home runs during his well-decorated career.

"The best way to describe Tewksbury, I always say, is that he was a comfortable oh-fer," McGriff says. "Because other pitchers that threw a whole lot harder, you've got to worry about how hard they're throwing, you may get hit, whatever. Tewks didn't throw very hard, you weren't intimidated, you weren't scared, nothing like that. Then at the end of the day, you were 0 for 4 and pissed off because how did you go 0 for 4 against this guy?

"He didn't throw very hard. He had great control. He threw strikes. He proves to you how hard it is to hit."

I became living proof that to thrive in the jungle that is major league baseball, a pitcher can elude the carnivores even while existing on their own turf. For thirteen seasons, I pumped strike after strike over the plate without ever risking a speeding ticket from the local authorities. And let me tell you, there are few things more satisfying in the world than eyeing a rival slugger eagerly step into the batter's box with hunger in his eyes, then watching him U-turn it back to the dugout with that look in those eyes having changed to fury. The kind of fury that Albert Belle once unleashed after he jammed himself with a 3 and 0 curveball. Up stepped Robin Ventura a couple of hitters later, with a message from Sir Albert to my catcher, Terry Steinbach: "Maybe Tewks had better get an escort to his car after the game, because Albert wants to kill him!"

From New York to Chicago to St. Louis and beyond, I pulled rabbits from the unlikeliest of hats, waved red capes at some of the game's most bullish sluggers and executed Houdini-like escapes from some of the toughest jams because I finally reached the point where I could see where I was throwing the baseball before I actually let go of it.

Sure, it takes physical acumen to throw strikes, the coordination and balance to build a repeatable delivery. A filthy fastball can make things easier because it allows a pitcher to miss spots and still get people out. But it's a two-part approach. The physical part is step two in the process. Step one happens upstairs, before a pitcher even winds up to throw the baseball. He must determine what pitch he is going to throw next and to which location to the plate, and once that part is finalized, the conviction must be there to throw it. Only then, when the conviction is forged in steely resolve, are the physical odds of throwing a strike to the desired location greatly increased. Conviction plus execution.

What I had done since the days of throwing to my chalk-outlined strike zone against the elementary school wall was imagine success in my mind and then begin the heavy-lifting physical process to get there. In so many ways, it was carrying out what I was reading all those years ago from my old friend Norman Vincent Peale. If you can conceive it in your mind, believe it in your heart, you can achieve it.

I was twenty-five when I had my Catfish encounter and I had figured out a few things by then but still had plenty of learning in front of me. Most importantly, I was changing from the inside out. Not that I was anywhere close to a finished product. The nomadic life of a ballplayer can leave both your body and your soul unmoored.

For example: One of the most difficult times I ever had leaving for spring training was in 1986, when I reported to my first major league camp with the Yankees and just a few weeks before my talk with Cat-fish. I had grown close with my youngest brother, Shawn, hanging out and going to movies. When departure day arrived, excited as I was for my first big-league camp, we said our goodbyes and hugged, and as I left to drive to Florida, I cried. Today, Shawn still carries a little indent between his eyes from where I nailed him with that base-ball when we were kids, and he always zings me with something like, "Yeah, great control. You missed the damn screen by a mile and hit me right between the eyes."

As I always tell players, thoughts become things. The hard work is in keeping those things positive. The game's great myth is that tal-ent ultimately triumphs. Sometimes, it absolutely does. But not ev-eryone is as talented as a Madison Bumgarner or Clayton Kershaw. For most of us, the talent is roughly equivalent, and the degrees of separation are very slight. That's where mental preparation and strength enter, stage right.

Without a strong foundation, success will be fleeting, or, even worse, elusive. All of us, in whatever line of work or whatever stage of life we are in, need a reference point to help us regain balance during troubled times, and a touchstone to continually fuel con-fidence for when things are going well. For me, those became my trained thoughts and my ability to throw strikes.

St. Louis is where I found steady ground and hit my stride and, looking back, the fact that I was near thirty when that happened was no accident. Each of us moves at his or her own pace. With-out that God-given lightning in my arm, my journey took a differ-ent path, one filled with experimentation, trial and error. As former big-leaguer Rick Reuschel once said, "I can't throw harder. But I can throw slower." A key part of my development was that I was able to grasp the presence of mind and develop a sense of self that eventu-ally allowed me the confidence to employ that philosophy.

Pitching in the major leagues is an incredibly difficult task, period, the degree of difficulty only ascending when you are without an overpowering fastball. Throwing strikes and excelling consistently without that in your toolbox is an art impossible for all but a few to master. Recognizing and understanding one's strengths and, especially, limitations, is enormously important in any aspect of life. By identifying that my best assets were my knack for pinpoint location and ability to change speeds, I eventually was able to take bigger steps forward.

The days of fleeing Rutgers because of homesickness a distant memory, I began to feel at home in St. Louis, the third stop in my career after the Yankees and Chicago Cubs. In 1990, left-hander John Tudor, who had finished second in NL Cy Young balloting in 1985 when he went 21-8 with a 1.93 ERA in thirty starts while pitching the Cardinals to that year's World Series against Kansas City, returned to St. Louis to finish his career. Tudor trafficked in slow-cooking, too. During that '85 season, he struck out only 169 batters in 275 innings yet still dominated. Despite the results, guys razzed John all the time about his soft-serve offerings. Tough guy that he was, Tudor never flinched, consistently hitting higher radar-gun readings with his answers than his fastballs. "Anyone can pitch throwing 95 to 98," Tudor would say. "It takes balls to pitch at 84 or 85." And, he would add, especially with no batting-practice L screen in front of you.

Tell me about it, and especially when Barry Bonds or Mark McGwire was at the plate. Those two were notoriously difficult to face and, later in their careers, of course, notorious for other reasons, too. Yes, I pitched smack in the middle of the steroids era, which simply was one more challenge in an MLB forest full of them. Basically, I did not know much about the game's subculture even during the height of it. I played next to Ken Caminiti in San Diego during his 1996

MVP season and I had no idea what he was doing nor, early, did I even suspect anything. Sure, there were moments in the spring when you would look at a guy and think, *Whoa, what kind of off-season program was he on?* But as it was with Cammy, there were some players who simply didn't look like they juiced. As for those who were suspected of juicing, what could you do? Performance-enhancing drugs weren't against baseball's rules at the time. For me, facing these artificially enhanced hitters, it was simply a matter of this: if that was something they wanted to do, then let them, but I can't worry about it. Whether they were taking androstenedione, creatine, Deca-Durabolin or just plain, good old-fashioned spinach, my task was still the same. Just throw strikes and get outs.

I kept a detailed journal in those days (something I recommend to players today), which helped me organize my thoughts and strategize against some of the game's greatest hitters. This, remember, was before the advent of laptop computers and video. All we had to go by was the advance reports our scouts filed, and if there were holes or gaps in those, it was up to me to fill them in. Because I didn't have a putaway fastball, my margin for error was much more slim than, say, that of Ryan or David Cone. So in my journal were detailed notes on hitters I would face. For example, one of my entries from sometime around 1993 for Bonds begins: "Fuck Bonds, start away—no matter if ball or strike, come in with high fastball at belt. He did not like this. Repeating this is important. Don't fall into patterns with him. He hit the FB away 2x." Another of my entries: "Start away, got away with 1-2 comeback sinker on inside part of plate. K (called)." When plan and execution sync up, life is good. When they don't, well, it usually means you get to shower early.

During one game in April 1996, when I was with the San Diego Padres, I got Bonds in his first at-bat to swing at a first-pitch fastball away, resulting in a fly ball to left field. Phew! That's about as easy a time as anybody ever had with Bonds, but those moments are fleeting. The bases were loaded in the fifth when Bonds next came to the plate, and the battle started all over again.

Based upon my own scouting reports and those of the league, I know down and away is a "safe" area in which to pitch Bonds early in the count. Add to that the fact that it worked so quickly and easily in Bonds's first at-bat, why not start him off with that? Ball one. Hmmm, was that first at-bat a mirage?

So Bonds now is ahead in the count 1 and 0, and I can read his mind from sixty feet, six inches away as easily as a large neon sign. He knows I do not have an overpowering fastball, so, in other words, he knows I possess no pitch he needs to worry about. Hitters did not need to be a modern-day Ted Williams to know the book on me is not complicated: throws a lot of strikes, doesn't throw hard, curveball is second-best pitch, likes to use it with runners in scoring position. Boom.

Bonds, of course, knows before he even steps to the plate that I can't throw the ball by him, so he can look for an off-speed pitch and still have time to react to the fastball. On the mound, I know Bonds has to be thinking, *This guy can't throw it by me inside, plus, he would be a dumbass if he tried.* Meanwhile, I know that if I throw a curve for the second pitch of the at-bat, Bonds probably will be "sitting" on that pitch—looking for it—the rest of the at-bat.

So I go with a slider down and in, something I never threw to left-handed hitters because it wasn't hard enough for a lefty to bite at and swing through. What it was was a clear case of me trying to outthink Bonds, show him something completely different, a pitch that carried the appearances of a fastball before breaking. Maybe it would tempt Bonds enough to swing, and he would either miss when the ball broke or swing over it and roll a grounder toward second base.

He rolled over nothing. Instead he squared up the ball and deposited it toward the Pacific Ocean. It was the only grand slam I ever allowed. Damn, should have walked him—which, to me, is like saying I should have swallowed some rat poison instead of those three Advil tablets for a headache. My whole game is staying away from walks. With Bonds, my intentions were good but, in reality, I was trying to fool one of the greatest hitters in the history of the game. Which isn't likely.

What really angered me, though, was Bonds's second homer an inning later.

Yes, walks were anathema to me, but I started the sixth inning by delivering a full-count walk to Giants pitcher Allen Watson. *What?!* You've got to be kidding me. Regrouping, I induced a ground ball from Marvin Benard that forced out Watson at second base. Then, I promptly balked Benard to second base.

Question: Where in the world was my mind at that point? How did I balk? Was I still thinking about that grand slam an inning earlier? Wait, that's three questions. All legitimate, too. Thoughts become things, and perhaps I had allowed these things to distract me, even ever so slightly. The problem is, in the major leagues, even the slightest of distractions for even a fraction of a second can lead to instant doom.

This is where both breathing and self-talk enter the equation. Aside from when the catcher trots to the mound or the pitching coach or manager visits, there are no time-outs in baseball. And that is why it is imperative for a player to be able to think his way through difficult situations. It starts with breathing. Slow that down, and everything else seems to slow down. Including the dialogue in your head, self-talk, that internal narrative we have about ourselves and what happens around us on a moment-by-moment basis. There is a direct relationship between our perceptions of ourselves and events around us. This is what determines self-talk. I call that voice the Little Man, the negative voice that hops onto your shoulder, out of the blue, seemingly at the most inopportune times and almost always right before you make a pitch. *Don't hang it! Don't walk him!* So what happens? Almost always, you wind up doing what you are trying not to do. When pitchers are doing well, they use positive self-talk. *I am going to throw a good fastball down in the zone* and *I am going to get a ground ball.* Things like that. And, yes, that's one more aspect of the mental game within the game. Working to control your self-talk, keeping it positive instead of negative.

So, with Benard on second, Robbie Thompson battled me to a full-count before I struck him out, bringing to the plate . . . Mr. Bonds, with two out, first base open and us trailing the Giants 6-4. Maybe the situation called for an intentional walk, but I am not walking him, not after that grand slam. I am getting this SOB out this time.

I start him with a curveball. In each of his first two at-bats, I started him with fastballs away. Now, with first base open and Matt Williams on deck, maybe he's thinking I will try to pitch around him. I'm thinking a curveball would be different, it's a change of pace, and if it becomes ball one, so what. Besides, I'm thinking he probably won't swing at the first pitch because most hitters avoid swinging at first-pitch curveballs, and if he thinks I'm pitching around him anyway . . . maybe I can "steal" a strike. "Stealing" a strike is what I like to call sneaking in a first-pitch strike because, if you can throw the ball over the plate, most hitters are not first-pitch swingers.

Barry Bonds, though, is not most hitters. And, he was sitting off-speed (meaning looking for an off-speed pitch instead of a fastball). Result: He took the pitch I intended to steal a strike with and knocked it to Carlsbad. Two innings later, I was in the showers and we would lose 9-4.

On some days, art and real life simply will not peacefully coexist. But, ah, the serendipitous days when they do, those are the ones that can make you feel like Superman. Just as I was finishing up an acrylic painting of Mark McGwire and Ken Griffey Jr. for charity in 1998 (each had agreed to sign a hundred prints), here came the St. Louis Cardinals into the Metrodome. It was the summer when

McGwire was smashing everything in sight and finished with a then single-season record seventy home runs. My catcher in Minnesota, Terry Steinbach, and I agreed to take my "eephus curveball" (a tantalizingly slow pitch traveling between 40 and 50 m.p.h.) out for a test drive if McGwire came up with nobody on base in the first inning.

This, you see, sprung directly from that grand bit of wisdom that those who do not study history are doomed to repeat it. McGwire for his career was 4 for 9 with one homer against me, and that homer had come the summer before when he was still playing in Oakland. During the pregame scouting meeting to go over how we would pitch to that night's lineup, Steinbach and I both agreed that I didn't have the fastball to pitch in on Big Mac. So in his second at-bat that night, the count 1 and 0, Steinbach signaled for a fastball away. I shook him off. So he called for a curveball away. I shook again. I'm thinking, *Mac's looking out over the plate now, or for something off-speed, so I can come in with a fastball and surprise him.* I didn't get the ball in and McGwire nearly decapitated the center-field cameraman with a monster home run.

Meantime, Steinbach obtained a new ball from the umpire and calmly walked it out to me. When he reached the mound, he simply dropped the ball into my waiting glove, lifted his mask so he could look me in the eye and said, "Well, Tewks, you didn't get that in, did you?" Then he turned and walked away, leaving me to deliver the next pitch to the next hitter through the thick fog of sarcasm.

That history lesson took. Now, my painting for charity nearly finished in the quiet of my home studio, here came McGwire roaring toward the Roger Maris home run chase into the oasis of my home ballpark. With word of our plan to throw the eephus to Mac if he batted in the first inning with the bases empty quickly spreading through our clubhouse, our relievers, who normally didn't descend the four flights of stairs (44 total!) from the clubhouse to the dugout until the second or third inning, gathered en masse. I should have charged them admission.

Sure enough, to the delight of our relievers who made the effort to clomp downstairs, McGwire did come to the plate with none on in that first inning.

Sure enough, I threw the eephus and it plopped into Steinbach's glove for a called strike. I threw it again and McGwire stepped . . . stepped again . . . wound up and coiled dramatically . . . whipped his bat around . . . and squibbed a slow roller to first. I ran toward the bag to cover and shot McGwire a look that, if you see the classic photo of the play, clearly says, "Oh no, are you going to beat me up for this?!"

Next time up, similar circumstances, eephus, again, for strike one, again. Now addicted, I threw another that McGwire popped to second. Though the strategy was honest, as nobody could tame Mc-Gwire that summer, it was the only time in my career I ever felt like an entertainer on the mound.

Still, the last thing I wanted was for McGwire to think I was trying to demean him, so after the game I sent a note over to the St. Louis clubhouse: "Mac, I hope you didn't think I was trying to embarrass you. Was just mixing up timing. Thanks again for signing the prints." McGwire, bless him, sent a note back: "I loved it. I am a sucker for those and would have swung at them all day."

Today, that note is framed, along with a picture of a photo from that game, and hangs on a wall in my house. And true to his note, McGwire chuckles at the memory. "I was always a location hitter so I looked location and I reacted to the ball. I looked for the hand, tried to pick up the hand and tried to understand what the grip was and I reacted to it. Especially with his curveball, it would pop up out of his fastball line. It popped up higher, and you could actually see it. It was just a matter of if you wanted to hit it. I always think back to those Bugs Bunny cartoons when that guy threw the eephus pitch and you had all those guys up there, 1-2-3 you're out! 1-2-3 you're out! I always thought about that when I faced him."

Retiring McGwire anytime you faced him, but especially on the ol' eephus? Priceless. But that acrylic painting that became a lithograph and was signed by McGwire and Griffey? We raised over $100,000 for the Boys & Girls Clubs of St. Louis, Seattle (Griffey's home city at the time) and Concord, New Hampshire.

Other hitters weren't always so gracious when encountering my eephus pitch. I broke it out on Willie McGee, my former teammate in St. Louis, when I was pitching for the Padres in 1996. McGee was a great player, an even better person and an exceptionally danger-ous switch-hitter. But separate friends into different teams, and let's not forget: this is fierce competition. There are major league egos, contracts to earn, families to feed, reputations to grow and maintain, pressure-cooker tension and heat-of-the-moment sparks.

I started McGee off with a first-pitch eephus and, curious, glanced up at the scoreboard as I readied for the next pitch. It read "46 m.p.h." As Willie often did, he stepped out while he was batting, removed his helmet and scratched the back of his neck with the brim. Next pitch? Fastball right down the middle for strike two. Again, I looked up at the scoreboard: "86 m.p.h." Having trapped McGee into an 0 and 2 hole, I fired another fastball, this one also 86 m.p.h., this one down and away. He took it for strike three.

The next day, Ozzie Smith confided that McGee was furious with me for embarrassing him. So I went looking for Willie, who initially refused to talk with me but, after some badgering, eventually did. I assured him: "Look, I promise, I wasn't trying to embarrass you. I was simply trying to get you out, and I need to change speeds to do that, and I wanted to get ahead with a curveball and this is how I sometimes have to do it."

I finally got him to cool off and, when he did, he laughed and said what I took as the highest of praise: "Tewks, I gotta tell you, after that first curveball, the next two pitches looked like they were a hundred miles an hour!"

Once I established myself in the bigs, my basic philosophy on the mound was pretty simple: I am either going to get the hitter or he is going to get me, but we aren't going to be here all day trying to figure it out. I hated to walk hitters. Related to that, I was never afraid of pitching to contact, which, I think, then and now, is the single biggest reason why pitchers don't throw the ball over the plate. They're afraid of what might happen, which is a negative way to think. I also preferred to work quickly because, among other things, it keeps your fielders and the plate umpire alert. I always figured the only people in the ballpark who don't like a fast-moving pitcher are the vendors, because it costs them hot dog and beer money. Otherwise, working quickly increases the chances of fielders making better plays behind you and umpires maybe giving you more borderline pitches.

Pitch location, versus pitch selection, is what makes or breaks a pitcher. No doubt, quality pitches are vital, but I've always believed pitchers need to throw the *right* pitch at the right time to really succeed. Pitching in a game is like constructing a thousand-piece jigsaw puzzle. Consider each pitch as one piece, and when they all fit together properly, you've really got something to look at.

Hall of Famer Greg Maddux was the master of this, which is why while preparing for a trip into Montreal just after Mad Dog's Atlanta Braves had passed through in 1994, I phoned him at his team hotel to pick his brain. Maddux was a rookie with the Cubs when I played for Chicago in 1987, so I had gotten to know him some, though not very well. But our styles were similar in that we both had to outthink that night's lineup.

Again, remember, these were the days before video scouting and saturation television coverage. In that world, I continued to seek out every possible advantage. So when Maddux phoned back after retrieving my message, we discussed the Expos lineup he had just faced and how to pitch certain hitters like Larry Walker, Moisés Alou, Marquis Grissom and Cliff Floyd. During the conversation, he mentioned that he always pitched to his strengths. Just like with Catfish, I had questions. What, exactly, did he mean?

"What pitch or pitches can you throw with confidence when you are *ahead* in the count?" Maddux asked. "What pitch or pitches can you throw when you are *behind* in the count? And what pitch or pitches can you throw when you are *even* in the count?"

The philosophy of ahead/behind/even. I had never considered this before in terms of pitch selection. But I found it pretty easy to answer. When I was ahead in the count, I could throw a fastball in or away, or a curveball under the strike zone. When I was behind in the count, I could throw a fastball away, or a curveball, or a changeup. When the count was even (1 and 1, 2 and 2), I would make a pitch based on the game situation and what pitches I threw to get to that count.

"Pitch selection within your comfort zone," Maddux says today, recalling our conversation. "It's a lot easier said than done. Hopefully, you've got more than one pitch you can throw in those situations. Hopefully, it's not the same pitch, unless it's really good. If it's a John Smoltz slider or Mariano Rivera cutter, if you've got an elite pitch like those, okay. But not many pitchers have that."

As far as our communication, Maddux chuckles regarding the shared conspiracy to outflank and outfox hitters.

"You talked to various players about teams you just faced," Maddux says matter-of-factly. "You'd steal their stuff and let them steal your stuff as far as how to pitch to hitters. I did it a lot with my brother Mike [now a pitching coach for the Washington Nationals] and other players around the league.

"You can watch guys pitch and get ideas, but to actually hear what they're seeing and why they're throwing certain pitches is a little different. You don't get why a guy threw a fastball up and in in a particular situation from watching on TV. You don't get the same picture as you do talking to pitchers about why they threw certain pitches in certain situations."

As I digested everything, what I discovered was this: Though I already knew this ahead/behind/even philosophy in basic, general terms, I had never really zeroed in on it. It had been mostly instinctual, which was helpful but vague. Armed with a sharpened focus after my conversation with Mad Dog, I went out and implemented this finely tuned pitch-to-pitch approach and earned a complete game, 4-1 victory. I was thirty-three at the time, still learning, still growing. Nothing came easy, and every bit of knowledge, including this from Maddux, was another arrow in my quiver.

"Tewks's strength as a pitcher was, he wasn't going to beat himself," Maddux says. "You were going to have to go out there and hit him. He wasn't going to walk you. He was going to throw strikes. He wasn't going to give in with his fastball. And when I say he was going to throw strikes, I mean both hard and soft with the fastball. He wasn't going to give you anything, you were going to have to earn every base. You weren't worried about working the count or even getting into a hitter's count. He wasn't overpowering. His mistake was going to be that he might catch a little more of the plate than he wanted."

Just throw strikes, kid.

Then: Which pitch can you throw with confidence when you are ahead in the count? Behind? Even?

Sometimes, knowledge comes replete with country philosophy and dripping in tobacco juice. *Splat!* Other times, it emanates from a professorial pitcher who veers toward the cerebral. There is no one size fits all.

And today, Maddux's reaction to my spinning some of this into my second career as a mental skills coach is priceless.

"Tewks is going to have a lot of street cred," Maddux says, his wicked sense for tossing off a hilarious one-liner still sharp as ever. "All the other mental skills coaches, their last sport, I think, was fourth-grade tetherball."

4

The Concrete Jungle

The view from the Yankee Stadium mound when Lou Piniella was managing and on his way to visit from the dugout, I imagine, could be much like that of a matador's inside a bull ring. And so it was in the fourth inning of a game against the Chicago White Sox in July 1987, when here came Piniella, stomping and snorting, and I was in trouble. The power of positive thinking? Let's just say I didn't sell him a pair of shoes that day.

As things turned out, this would be the last of my thirty-one appearances (26 starts) over two seasons for the Yankees. The talk with Catfish Hunter the previous spring was inspiring. Camp that year was thrilling. I threw twenty consecutive scoreless innings, after which I was named as the camp's outstanding rookie and as the Yankees' fourth starter. I won my first major league start, a 3-2 decision over Milwaukee. Many family and friends traveled to the Bronx from New Hampshire for the occasion. Afterward, a present from Yankees owner George Steinbrenner was waiting at my locker: a bottle of champagne that seemed as tall as the Statue of Liberty.

To this day, I keep that bottle, still unopened, at home in my trophy case among assorted team jerseys and various autographed baseballs and pictures. Here's the thing about playing in New York, though: The wily genies have a way of escaping even unopened bottles to torment you. Though I went 9-5 with a 3.31 ERA in twenty-three games (20 starts) during my rookie season, I was out of the rotation and in the bullpen by June, shipped back to Triple-A Columbus by July and then called back again. Too often as I whipsawed back and forth, I was dogged by the fear of failure. Always, it lurks just around the next corner in the major leagues; that's just life at this level. But New York, and especially playing for the Yankees, exacerbates the feeling. Another minor league demotion always seemed just one poor performance away. I was dispatched to Triple-A Columbus temporarily again early in '87. The thing is, when you go, you don't know that it's going to be temporary. It could be permanent, your last chance at the major leagues ripped away like a dying man's last grab at oxygen.

All of this plays into the mind games of the major leagues, which is why the more you can control your breathing, slow things down and persist in reinforcing yourself by visualizing positive mental images, the healthier and happier you will be. Even when you're doing well, especially early in a career, you're never quite sure you have a permanent foothold. In essence, I felt like I was back at Rutgers having to claw my way back up. In part, that experience gave me the confidence to know I could do it again. But what I didn't know at the time were the challenges still ahead and how long it would take to overcome them.

My third major league start was in Kansas City against a Royals team just two years removed from winning the World Series and featuring Hall of Famer George Brett. I took a shutout into the middle innings that day, which is where things got quite interesting. Ahead of Hal McRae 0 and 2, I threw a hard fastball up and in, which made him uncomfortable and caused plate umpire Larry McCoy to issue me a warning. It still mystifies me as to why. Maybe it was because I was a rookie and hadn't earned my stripes yet. Whatever, all I knew was this: the inside part of the plate effectively had been taken away, because post-warning, if I hit somebody or came too far inside, I would be ejected.

Nevertheless, I was able to slip an inside fastball by McRae for a called strike three on the next pitch and then, in the seventh inning, I wound up hitting Willie Wilson in the shoulder with another 0 and 2 pitch. This time, Wilson hollered at me, took a few steps toward the mound, pointed, yelled some more and then started running toward me. Three starts into my career, and my first bench-clearing brawl. Thanks to our corner infielders, Don Mattingly and Mike Pagliarulo, Wilson never reached me. Still, there was a pileup and I wound up at the bottom, jamming the middle finger on my pitching hand so I had to be removed from the game. We won 5-1, and afterward, I headed for the team bus.

This should have been the difficult part of the day, right? Not so fast. The Kauffman Stadium elevators are located just outside both clubhouses, so it is not uncommon for players from both teams to wind up in a sort of unintended "mix zone." As if in a scene from a movie, as I was waiting for the elevator to take us up, just as the doors started to close, who should hurry in but the great Brett himself. I had struck him out on a changeup during the game, by the way, which was a pretty exciting moment for me.

Now, talk about nervous and awkward. When I was seven years old and playing youth league baseball for Concord Group Insurance in New Hampshire, I became so anxious before games that I once peed my pants. True story. And this wasn't even with George Brett growling at me inside an elevator. Fears: At any age, we have them, and we've got to face and overcome them.

"Hey, kid," Brett snarled. "Gotta be careful pitching inside. You could get someone hurt."

This guy was a god among men in the game. I was a lowly rookie. How was I even supposed to respond? I was speechless.

Then, before I even uttered a sound, Brett added this: "Great job. Don't ever stop pitching inside."

The elevator doors opened, and I started breathing again.

So I knew some of what I had to do to survive in the majors, in theory. But so many things come at you so quickly, it is easy (and natural) to become overwhelmed and confused before you even know what hit you. Essentially, being a rookie pitcher in New York is similar to being an antelope in the African desert. You're waiting to become somebody's meal.

By 1987, it felt like the walls were closing in around me. Every bit of turbulence seemed magnified. With every poor outing, my self-doubt and fear increased and the press speculated that I would be the next player to be shipped out. Without a mental skills coach, I suffered alone. I really didn't have anyone to share my thoughts with, nor was I sure in those days and in that New York atmosphere that I really wanted to talk to anybody, even if I had someone around.

After one poor outing in Fenway Park, as I was having my post-game dinner, I overheard a clubhouse attendant remark that in all of his years in the game, he could not recall someone getting knocked around as badly as me and then gorging so exuberantly afterward. These are the kinds of offhand comments that really can worm their way into your head, and stay there. They also are the kind of comments that reinforce why, as a player, you need to develop a strong mental garbage disposal that can simply grind up words like those and make them disappear. Your mental health should neither be subject to, nor dependent upon, the uninformed or cruel opinions of others.

In baseball, as in life, your own doubts and fears are constantly reinforced, rightly or (mostly) wrongly, by those around you. It takes time, and maybe the help of others, to reach the point where your foundation is strong enough to withstand the barrage of constant negative reinforcement. I battled it as a player, and now, through years of hands-on experience and lots of study, I help today's players battle similar, age-old issues. Insecurity is more rampant than seventh-inning stretches in this game.

In New York when I first started to struggle, I had coaches telling me all kinds of things to work on. Don't get me wrong, it's great that they cared. But at the same time, I'm not sure my struggles were fundamental flaws in my mechanics. Although my shoulder was beginning to feel the effects of a big-league workload, I mostly felt okay physically. The majority of my struggles were in my mind. My confidence was low. I was distracted by outside influences. So many thoughts were coming at me. How do you tell your pitching coach, or your manager, that you've lost confidence? What would he say, or do? Suffering alone is no way to go, not then, not today, not ever. But as I tried to figure things out, that's what I did.

This is where the conflicting emotions of a minor league demotion make themselves known. One day after being yanked from a start after only two innings to begin the 1987 season, I was back in the bullpen and called upon to pitch another 2.1 innings for Piniella's Yankees. Back-to-back days, a start and then a relief appearance! When I look back at that, it's utter insanity. No wonder I was so anxious, nervous and afraid. Four days later, I started again and surrendered three runs in 3.2 innings. I was at a loss as to how to get back on track, and I suspected my next chance to figure it out would be in the minor leagues.

Sure enough, I was handed my papers for Triple-A Columbus, and it may have been the only time I was excited to go back to the bushes. I had reached the point where I couldn't handle the pressure to perform at the major league level. My stomach churned each day I came to the park wondering what would happen next. Another start? A demotion to the bullpen? Would this be the day they sent me down?

I knew going back to the minors would give me a chance to regain what I had lost on the mound. I would simply go back to starting, without the worry of being yo-yoed between the rotation and the bullpen or anything else. And yet, not being in control of your own destiny as a player eats at you, too. I knew that even if I was lights out over my next couple of starts, it wouldn't guarantee a return trip to Yankee Stadium.

In one sense, it felt good to be back among familiar faces and some of my friends in the minor leagues. And I knew I at least didn't have to worry about being demoted further, to Double-A, so I could just go out and pitch. Yet in another sense, it was still Triple-A, the difference between a Lamborghini and a Ford Pinto. My demotion in '87 lasted about two months, and early on there were times when I snarled. Once, my manager, Bucky Dent, yanked me early from a game and I tossed my glove under the bench and grumbled that getting removed in the fourth inning "is not what I'm here for." To which Dent quickly walked over and sternly told me: "Well, I'm trying to win games and that performance stunk!" As I stewed, a teammate I respected sidled up to me and said, "You're not in New York, you're HERE! That was horseshit, Tewks!"

Stunned, I started to snap back to reality. I appreciated my teammate's comments. I needed to hear them. My pissed-off stage lasted about a week. Once I started focusing *not* on getting back to the majors—at least, once I removed that thought from the forefront of my mind—I started pitching better. By mid-June, I was back in New York, though I would lose three of my next four decisions with the Yankees while being unable to consistently keep my mind working in a productive direction.

And so it was on July 9, 1987, the bubbly gift from Steinbrenner barely a year old, the sands of my New York hourglass rapidly draining, that I devised a plan before my start at the Stadium against the White Sox. I walked out to the bullpen with my pitching coach, Mark Connor, to warm up before the game, having mustered as much false bravado as I could at the time. All week, I had paid a little too much attention to the chattering New York media, which swore that with one more poor outing, I would be shipped out to Columbus yet again.

So I took a Sharpie to the inside bill of my game-day cap, and as "Goose" Connor and I reached the bullpen for pregame warm-ups, I removed the cap, turned it upside down and proudly showed him that I had scribbled "Nothing to lose." He simply nodded. That wasn't exactly the show of encouragement I was looking for and, looking back, who knows what he was thinking. He was probably worried about his own job (another little-known secret about major league life: this generally is what everyone—players, coaches and managers—is most worried about most of the time). But from a distance, I can quickly identify what I was thinking with that stunt. In my neophyte efforts to be brave and focus on a positive, I was actually fueling my negative thoughts and fears.

By writing "Nothing to lose," I was focusing on exactly the negative result I was afraid of: losing.

Or, Lou-sing? It was the fifth inning that day when Piniella came stomping and snorting to the mound. I had shaken off my catcher,

Mark Salas, and thrown a changeup that Harold Baines drilled for an RBI single that erased our lead and tied the game at 2-2.

"Why the hell did you call for a changeup?" Piniella demanded from Salas.

I spoke up, defending my catcher.

"He didn't," I explained. "I shook to it."

Piniella's head snapped around in a flash of anger.

"Well, son, what the hell," Piniella snapped. "That's not how you pitch this guy. You better get this guy out or I'm taking you out of the game."

"Fine."

Talk about your basic, sobering moments in life. This one conversation on the mound illustrates the fragile state of a roster spot in the major leagues, especially in New York, and especially for young players.

I proceeded to throw the next couple of pitches as hard as I could to Iván Calderón, and he proceeded to smash another base hit up the middle. Later, I would learn that there are three styles of pitching: prayer, perfect and primal. Prayer happens when a pitcher has no confidence in his stuff on a particular day and is just throwing pitches up there praying for hitters to make an out. Perfect happens in a couple of different ways: one when the pitcher gets ahead of the hitter and then tries to make the perfect pitch, often resulting in deep counts; and it happens when a pitcher has no confidence in his ability and tries to make the perfect pitch each time, usually resulting in the pitcher falling behind right away 1-0, 2-0 and so on. Primal is just trying to throw the ball as hard as you can. This usually happens when a pitcher is angry and opts for power with no consideration for anything but intensity.

During the Calderón at-bat, I was in pure primal mode. And true to his word, Piniella was out of the dugout practically before the ball landed in the center-field grass. I was gone.

Gone, as in, for good. I was out of that game, dropping my record to 1-4 with a 6.75 ERA in New York in 1987, and I was out of the Yankees' plans. Four days later, during the All-Star break, they shipped me, Rich Scheid and Dean Wilkins to the Chicago Cubs for left-handed pitcher Steve Trout.

I learned some pretty harsh lessons during this time that would help me both then and in the future. One, I had better both construct and refine my mental edge, and quickly. Two, true fearlessness, while admittedly difficult to achieve, is something much more than a Hallmark-inspired slogan written onto the bill of your cap.

For a pitcher, Piniella was neither an easy nor a soothing influence. Like many New Englanders, I vividly recalled the play he made in right field during the 1978 Yankees–Red Sox one-game playoff in which he snared a ball on one hop that he didn't see off the bat. Playing right field during day games in Fenway Park always has been a challenge, and I asked Lou once in the spring of 1986 how in the world he made the play. "Every blind squirrel finds an acorn now and again," he cracked.

Compounded, undoubtedly, by the pressure of managing in New York, Piniella, whose background was as a hitter, never did have much patience for pitchers, especially for one like me. Certainly, he wasn't blind to the fact that I didn't throw hard. After 20 scoreless innings in the spring of '86 and 7-plus innings and a victory in my first major league start, I gave up ten hits in 6.1 innings to Cleveland in my second start. Piniella didn't let the opportunity pass, telling me, "Bobby, you're not going to stay around long if you keep giving up ten hits a game."

Though I was 5-1 with three complete games (including one in a nifty seventy-five pitches) against the Reds with Lou managing, and he couldn't have been blind to that, either, I was handed my walking papers. Which, initially, is what a trade feels like. The knee-jerk human reaction is to view it through the prism that your current team does not want you, rather than you are a desired commodity by your new team. Again, with the pervasive negativity that can corrode a career before it gets going.

Adding insult to the injury of the first trade of my career was the bombastic Steinbrenner famously crowing to Piniella after the deal that in acquiring the veteran lefty Trout, "I just won you the pennant."

Another lesson in not letting others determine your own self-worth. While Trout was a fine pitcher over twelve seasons, going 88-92 with a 4.18 ERA for the White Sox, Cubs, Yankees and Seattle Mariners, he never won a game for the Yanks.

Instead, he went 0-4 with a 6.60 ERA in fourteen games (9 starts) for the Yankees in '87. Not only did he not win the pennant for the Yankees, why, I'm guessing he never even got a bottle of champagne from Steinbrenner.

5

Fear and Loathing
on the Mound

The boss's kiss-off still ringing loudly in my ears, I couldn't have been more eager to turn the page, author my next chapter and prove to Steinbrenner, Piniella and the rest of the Bronx Bombers that they had bombed in the worst way. In the way that they handled me, with their impatience, by giving up on me, everything. They had just bought the pennant by *trading* me? Yeah, I would definitely show them.

And then this little toothache feeling deep within my right shoulder blew up with the pressure of a thousand root canals.

There is a reason why you so often hear following a trade that maybe it will be a good thing for a player involved because a "fresh start" will send him off in a better direction. I didn't know much about the Chicago Cubs organization other than, at the time, Wrigley Field had no lights and I thought it would be pretty cool to play day games in one of my favorite cities and have nights at home. And having been shuttled between Triple-A and the majors and between the New York rotation and bullpen for seemingly an interminable amount of time, the artist in me was eagerly anticipating a clean slate, new drawing tools and the chance to show some fresh eyes a finished portrait.

But in a game that preys on every single fear and insecurity a player has, and then zeroes in on a few he doesn't even know he has, here's another one. I reported to Chicago's Triple-A club in Iowa figuring it would be just a short stopover en route to the majors, when my shoulder started to hurt in a way that told me I was injured, not simply sore. I continued to pitch anyway, because I was the new guy in town and I didn't want people to think I was soft. Plus, what I wanted most of all in that moment was to be able to stay on the mound, find my rhythm and prove I could contribute.

Finally, during an afternoon game in Rochester, New York, against the Baltimore Orioles' Triple-A club, my shoulder was hurting badly enough that I phoned the Cubs' farm director afterward and asked to see the team doctor. Sorry, he said, we can't get you in for a couple of weeks.

Thoroughly frustrated with both my pitching performance and the state of my shoulder, I picked up the phone and dialed Dr. Arthur Pappas. At the time, Pappas was the Boston Red Sox team physician and *the* guy in the industry, and I was fortunate enough to have known him through New England baseball circles. We can get you in on Monday, his office told me, so I phoned the Cubs' farm director back, passed on that piece of news and suddenly, magically, he was able to get me an appointment with the Cubs' team doctor early the next week.

What the Cubs doctor told me was that tests showed I needed surgery to shrink the capsule in my right shoulder, a relatively new procedure at the time that was just coming into vogue. I thanked him, added that I wanted to get a second opinion and then went off to see Dr. Pappas. I braced myself, fearing the worst, and his recommendation came back. Rest and rehabilitation and let's see how things go.

Now, there are many, many people in your ear as a major league baseball player: managers, pitching coaches, hitting coaches, teammates, friends on rival teams, friends from back home, family members, writers, broadcasters, the cast of characters goes on and on and on. Usually, they mean well, and sometimes, their advice is good. Always, though, it can cause excess noise in your head. It is imperative to stay on high alert and sift through it all quickly and, ultimately, understand that you are the one responsible for your own career. I learned this lesson long ago and it is another one I pass along to players I coach today. For me, I was done with rest and rehab. I wanted to be fixed, and I wanted to be fixed now, and so Dr. Pappas agreed to perform exploratory surgery in July 1988.

He repaired a torn labrum at the UMass Memorial Medical Center in Boston, and I remember waking up in my hospital room with my girlfriend, Laura, waiting by the bed. Soon, we were off to the wonderful world of rehabilitation and, fortunately, mine would not be quite as bumpy as the ride home from the hospital. We were staying with my best buddy and his wife in a little town called Webster, New Hampshire, and as Laura drove down the dirt road toward their home and my uncertain future, every single bump jostled the sling protecting my arm, sending waves of agony shuddering throughout my body. When we finally arrived, Laura and our friends mixed a couple of drinks and proceeded to enjoy the evening. Not wanting to be left out, I asked for one, too. Plus, my shoulder was a mess and my career was in a downward spiral, so why not? Mistake. A cocktail or two, combined with the painkillers already in my body, sent the room spinning. I remember telling Laura: "I'm not sure having that drink was a good idea. Will you check on me later to make sure I'm still breathing?"

She'd done a pretty good job of that for a few years to that point, and she's done an excellent job of it in all the years since. Breathe in. Breathe out. Slowly and calmly. Now, step into what's next. Together in life, for both of us as we've raised our two wonderful, college-graduate children and for me on the mound.

WE MET DURING the fall of 1985. I had just been put on the Yankees' forty-man roster and was living with that same best buddy, Dale, who would be the best man at our wedding, and his wife. They had moved from the "sticks" of New Hampshire to Concord just after my debut with the Yankees. I was in a good place. I was just off of a great month with Triple-A Columbus and was back home, driving around in my two-tone, brown Mercury Zephyr and without any significant concerns involving trades, rehabilitation or much else beyond what I would throw for my next strike. My high school catcher, Tim Hoyt, had loaned me money so I didn't have to work in the off-season. I could just focus on my workouts, and I would pay him back with my first major league check. Talk about a great time in your life.

One night, I had a blind date set up with one of my sister's friends, but when I went to pick her up, she wasn't there. So I headed for a beer at a place called B. Mae Denny's. I was sitting at the bar, watching television, when I noticed a very attractive woman passing by. We made eye contact and, moments later, I was invited by another gal to join a group of men and women gathered in a corner of the bar. I did and, a few minutes later, presto, I was talking with Laura, the woman I'd watched walk by. We had a sandwich, which she paid for, which immediately got the minor-leaguer in me thinking, *This woman has money!* Oh, the things in life you remember.

She was with me at a resort in the Catskills during the All-Star break in 1987 when, as we checked in, the bellhop informed me that I had been traded to the Cubs. Ah, life before the trusty smartphones, or even the rudimentary early cell phone. I guess the Yankees had no way to reach me, so sometimes that's the way it worked in the majors, too. A guy finds out he's traded for the first time in his life in some fairly entertaining (and, possibly, incomprehensible) way. You simply hang with 'em and control the parts of life you can control.

Laura and I were married in January 1989, in Concord, New Hampshire, just after she finished her MBA at Boston University and just after we purchased our first house, the small Cape Cod design on the south end of town. She had a great job at a hospital as an assistant to the president, and it afforded her some flexibility to visit me that March after I signed with the St. Louis Cardinals as a free agent.

For me, this all meant I was moving into another stage of my career, one that I readily identify to players I coach today. None of us stays the same. As the years roll by, we grow into different stages of ourselves, taking on new responsibilities and identities. We add more layers to our lives. As I worked to get my shoulder back into shape, I was no longer that young boy with a baseball in one hand and a dream in the other. Not everything was about me and only me anymore. As I strengthened my shoulder, the responsibility of paying a mortgage and of eventually having a growing family began to take root. More thoughts. More potential crises of confidence. More what-ifs and unknowns straight up ahead.

Especially, more need for the imagery practice that had become a focal point of my preparation through the tumult of the Yankees years. I not only continued using it as my anchor, I worked on ways to build on it. Mental imagery incorporates visualization, motor imagery, mental practice and mental rehearsal. Some of this has caused confusion among coaches, athletes and even researchers, who have described it as "internalized rehearsal involving precise multisensory representation of the athletic experience." Translation: Seeing and feeling yourself in your mind perform an athletic skill or activity before you actually do it. It stimulates an inner feeling of action, producing responses both physiological and emotional. When an athlete replicates an on-the-field experience vividly in his or her mind, he or she actually can feel like they're performing.

The benefits are immense. Among them are increased confidence, controlled emotions, improved focus, sharpened concentration, an increased ability to correct errors, and learning and refining skills. When an unwanted situation occurs in a game and the player already has prepared with mental imagery, calm should replace a fear of the unknown or even panic, and instead the thinking goes, *Ah, I've been here before. I've got this.*

Seven months after a surgery that Dr. Pappas, at my retirement party years later, would admit could have ended my career, my shoulder was coming along okay. But in the spring, I had good days and bad days. I still remember sitting on the aluminum bleachers, on one of Laura's visits, at the minor league complex following the workout and telling her: "The way I feel right now, I may be home soon." My arm ached and I wasn't sure whether I could even get through the spring. And I was certain that if I didn't pitch better or regain my health, my career might be finished.

Visit that place too often, and it can lead down darkened, scary, dead-end paths. Because just as positive imagery can lead to improved performance, focusing on negative images can easily erode that performance. Get too deep into the middle of an inning that is starting to go sideways, surrender a two-run double and greet that moment with a reaction along the lines of "Dammit, I KNEW that was going to happen!" and I'll show you a pitcher who is not going to produce the tools to stop the bleeding.

I kept working on the field, and I kept my imagery exercises going off of it. As the shoulder improved, so, too, did the confidence of my Triple-A manager Mike Jorgensen. He allowed me to progress slowly, I broke camp as one of the Louisville Redbirds' starters and I went 13-4. That September, when rosters expanded, I got called up to the big club and, one week later, I was starting for the Cardinals in a pennant race, facing the Expos in Montreal. It was exciting in so many ways, battling back to the majors, regaining that sense of great accomplishment and, not the least of which, it meant a month of big-league salary, too. Pretty sweet for a newly married couple. Maybe we were going to be able to afford our new house after all.

Except . . . despite my dominant, thirteen-win season in 1989, I absorbed another blow when the Cardinals sent me back to Louisville at the end of the next spring to start the 1990 season. I had rehabbed my shoulder. Produced on the field. Contributed to the Cardinals' pennant race. I was in a good place mentally. And then, *boom!*

A few weeks into the season, I was doing my running in the outfield before a game when I encountered Ken Rowe, who had been my pitching coach in Triple-A with the Yankees organization. Like most Triple-A players, I had a sharp tendency to evaluate the major-leaguers just above me and wistfully say and believe I could be doing the same thing. So I not only told Ken that, but I fingered one of the mid-rotation guys with my old Yankees club, Andy Hawkins. "I can do what Andy's doing," I told Ken. And I've never forgotten his sharp response: "Then go ahead and do it!"

Tricky proposition right there, because how the hell do you do that when you're stuck in the minors? This is the conundrum hundreds and hundreds of players face each summer. Results on the field are one thing, but so many other factors figure into the equation as well. The construction of the big-league roster that might have no room at your position, opportunity, the prejudices of a coach or a manager, luck . . . so many things. Yet this also is where ability combined with sharp mental skills play large, because if you give in to the whole "woe is me, nobody will give me a fair shake" thoughts, then all of that negative reinforcement can lead straight to a self-fulfilling prophecy. And you'll be home killing time at Starbucks wondering whatever happened to your career before you know it.

So I challenged Ken—not exactly the illustration of a calm and cool mental game in that particular moment. "How do I do it?" I demanded. He explained very calmly: "When you get the chance, you prove it."

That chance arrived a few weeks later in St. Louis, under Whitey Herzog's direction, between the crusty Ted Simmons and the Busch Stadium concrete wall, when I was told that I was getting the ball, and if I did well, there would be another start, and if not, well, nobody could be sure what would happen.

Imagery and breathing foundations in place, I relaxed and succeeded. Things had not gone as well as I would have liked in Chicago, but I gained my balance and consistently reached for the stars in St. Louis and then subsequently in stops in Texas, San Diego and Minnesota. Joe Coleman, my pitching coach in St. Louis in '90, earned my gratitude forever with his help in a mechanical adjustment that brought my arm angle down to a three-quarter-level delivery following my shoulder surgery, a strategic weapon that helped save my shoulder by not pinching it so much with the higher arm-slot. It was a mechanical move that helped me to refine my strike-throwing ability to an even sharper degree. And Herzog's successor as field manager in St. Louis, Joe Torre, was an enormous boost to my confidence.

My modest velocity had become even more modest, post-shoulder surgery. But I could visualize what I was going to do in my next start, I was mastering the art of pinpoint control and over the next several seasons, it all came together. Against hitters like Andrés Galarraga, Hal Morris, Tim Salmon and Moisés Alou, I served fair warning: If you were going to beat me, it was going to be on my pitch, not your pitch.

Salmon, the old California Angels slugger, became one of the few hitters who solved me more often than not, going .538 (7 for 13) with one homer and four RBIs in his career against me. Today, Salmon smiles while recalling the challenges.

"He was the kind of pitcher where those were the toughest games to play," Salmon says, his success notwithstanding. "Not because of the stuff he had, but because you knew you were going to be in this emotional cat-and-mouse contest the whole night, trying to stay one pitch ahead of the game. And this might sound foreign in today's game because I don't think you see as much of it, but back then you had pitchers like him that you couldn't just go up and say, 'Hey, they're going to throw a fastball and go get 'em.' They had a bigger zone to work with, they knew how to manipulate the ball and work both sides of the plate, up and down. They were going to make you go up there and they weren't going to make many mistakes. You had to go up there and almost think along with them and hunt that zone where they were going to throw the ball next. That was the challenge that made guys like Tewks tough to face and made him the pitcher he was.

"You think about Greg Maddux, same kind of thing. When I think of him, I put him in that category of players where sometimes it was much easier to face the guy who was going to throw 94 or 95 because he was going to throw one or two pitches and he was going to give you enough looks at the fastball and he was going to make mistakes. Guys like Bob, you weren't going to get those kind of pitches.

"I was a guy who liked to play the cat-and-mouse. Literally, the guys who threw 95 were above my speed limit."

Alou, on the other hand, batted .133 (4 for 30) in thirty-three life-time plate appearances. Two of the four hits were homers, and in my journal I noted that use of the curveball was good against him. He says he did not try to think along with me because he was so young and hadn't figured a lot of things out yet, and there's one more example of where you can find a mental edge, exploiting a hitter's inexperience, if you have the diligence to keep looking. I did.

"I remember he didn't throw 95, he didn't have a surreal slider, but I could not get hits off of this guy," Alou says. "If you see my stats against him, they're really bad. And one of the few times I got a hit off of him I tried to make it a double and I broke my leg at first base. Rounding first base, I dislocated an ankle, one of the ugliest injuries that ever happened in MLB. That's how bad my memories are against Tewksbury."

Not everything was foolproof, of course. Is it ever? Whether on the field or in life, just when you think you have a few things figured out, something comes along to show you that no, you don't. You've still got work to do. Salmon was one of those. So was Jay Bell (career .339, 20 for 59, against me) and Hall of Famer Ryne Sandberg (.341, 15 for 44, .362 on-base percentage). It's been said that the pitcher's mound can be the loneliest place on the planet, and when a hitter steps into the box who has had fairly good success against you during his career, it's true, at times you can feel stranded and naked all alone out there on the mound. Not that you ever back down from a challenge. You just keep trying to outguess the hitter, gathering more and more information as you go, and the fact that all of them have their own unique, individual approaches against you always keeps it interesting.

"I just wanted to know what the pitcher had," says Sandberg, whom you now can find in Cooperstown, New York, during Hall of Fame weekend each July. "I knew what Tewks featured. He was with the Cardinals and we were playing each other all the time, so you got more familiar with him. I also think that back then, teams would see pitchers more often because there were only two divisions and you played so many games within your division. That's when it was more of a cat-and-mouse game between pitchers and hitters, and that's when if you're not having success, you have to do something different, and now it's back and forth. Often back then the schedule was, we'd have to face a pitcher within our division and then we'd see them again two or three weeks later. I'd go do my homework mentally. *Okay, this is what happened, now let's see in tonight's first at-bat what he's thinking right here.*"

As Sandberg says, he and I have kidded about some of our battles in the years since. As is the case with so many other hitters over the years, reviewing all of the little battles that made up the bigger wars, each of us recalls our individual triumphs in vivid high definition, and we recall our bruising defeats with head-shaking regret regarding how our approach in that one instance could have been different.

"I would say that when I had success against a certain pitcher, it would be a past history that started that snowball rolling," Sandberg says, noting one of the universal truisms of sport: success breeds confidence, and it can feed on itself. "That's a confidence builder, and it must also have to do that what the pitcher throws agrees with my swing. Tewks had a fastball that would come in to a right-handed hitter; for the most part, if it was outside it would come in to the bat or if it was inside it would come farther inside. And I was an inside-fastball hitter."

Rereading my journals from that time today, I noted clearly to myself: "Sandberg wants the ball middle-in. So go inside off the plate against him, then follow that up with fastballs and breaking balls away."

"I would often see that inside pitch," Sandberg says. "It wouldn't always be the first one, sometimes it was the second pitch, or third pitch, but I'd see it somewhere in the at-bat because he had to throw a fastball and that was usually the pitch I would do damage on. And I think that snowballs into so much confidence: 'Okay, I can hit his fastball, I'm on his fastball, now when he throws a slow curveball the confidence is still there and I'm able to have success.'"

Looking back at my journals, interestingly, I read an entry from September 18, 1992, after Sandberg went 2 for 2 with a walk. His first at-bat that day was a four-pitch walk (what?!), then he cracked a two-run homer in his second at-bat and a double in his third. From my journal entry at that point: "Hit the SOB! [curveball] down away, hadn't thrown many to him this year. When you come in, go in hard and if you hit him you hit him! When going in throw the two-seam so it moves into him. Need movement in." I found something very interesting after this game. I faced the Cubs three times in '93, and he played in only two of the games and was 0 for 8. In '94, I pitched against the Cubs twice and he didn't play. In '94, I faced him only once and he was 0 for 3 and I hit him in his second at-bat. I guess I finally got the ball in. Bottom line: After that September 18 game, Ryno was 0 for 11 against me.

As for Sandberg's Cubs, one of my most memorable moments involving them actually came not while I was playing for them, but after my liftoff in St. Louis. We were set to host the Cubs for a series late in the 1991 season, and I had arranged for a friend to fly in to drive my car home. He was flying into St. Louis on the afternoon of the first game of the series with the Cubs, and I was scheduled to start. So my first task was to meet my buddy at the airport, and I was waiting for him at the gate (something you were able to do in those days of innocence before 9/11) when some of the passengers began to disembark. As I stood there, I started to recognize some of the people emerging from the plane . . . and their employer kept offices on the north side of Chicago, on Clark and Addison Streets. Yep, here came the Cubs: Ryne Sandberg . . . Andre Dawson . . . Shawon Dunston . . . Mark Grace . . . broadcasters Harry Caray and Steve Stone. Not only could you wait at the gate in those days, but for some reason the Cubs that day flew commercial rather than taking the usual charter flight customary for major league clubs.

Quickly, I stepped back from the gate to try to blend in with the crowd and avoid an up-close meeting with my near-term opponent. My friend eventually exited and I headed to the ballpark. Later that day, during batting practice, I crossed paths with Cubs radio broadcaster Ron Santo, the Hall of Famer who sadly passed away a couple of years ago.

"Hey, Tewks," Santo quipped, "I knew we were going bad, but when the opposing pitcher comes to meet you at the airport, you know you're *really* struggling."

Truth be told, if I had known the Cubs were coming in, I would have had a limo pick up Sandberg and deliver him far, far away, perhaps to one of those country music theaters on the other side of Missouri, in Branson. And that night, sure enough, he cracked a solo homer against me in the sixth inning. But wait, there's more. I retired him in his three other at-bats (ground ball to first, ground ball to third and strikeout), earned the win in a 5-4 game, locked in my 1991 record at 11-12 with a 3.25 ERA and moved well beyond the shoulder surgery that two years earlier had threatened my career.

The bumpy ride post-surgery had given way, finally, to the smooth sailing and mental fearlessness that would lead to my All-Star season in 1992. And the talk with Laura while sitting on the aluminum bleachers in spring training of 1990, the one in which I feared I might be home soon, would become just one more lesson in the syllabus I use today to help players confront their own inner doubts and demons.

6

Nearly Perfect

Things always are changing in this game; targets always moving. And so it was one night in Philadelphia with the late Doug Harvey behind the plate. Known simply as "God" during his thirty-year career as an umpire that would lead to his eventual induction into the Hall of Fame, Harvey's authoritative presence and interpretation of the rules were legendary, which led to that all-powerful nickname. His was the final word. Add to this his impeccable manner, from perfectly coiffed hair to perpetually crisp uniform, and no umpire was more highly respected.

On this night, I was doing my best Muhammad Ali rope-a-dope impersonation, battling through allowing baserunners in each of the first four innings. Making matters more tricky, this was a season in which umpires were under pressure from the league to make sure pitchers came to a complete stop when working from the stretch—something that had never been really emphasized. Before, the pitcher could go into his set, get the sign from the catcher, come up without stopping and deliver the pitch.

So as I was walking off the field after the fourth inning, Harvey met me at the foul line, lifted his mask and said, "Son, you've got to give me a better stop than that or I'm going to have to balk you."

As he was talking to me, I happened to look down and notice that his zipper was undone. Knowing Doug was a proper man, never an item of clothing out of place, I couldn't resist. "Doug," I told him, "I'll come to a complete stop when you zip up your fly."

Doug was taken aback. Flustered, he turned toward the field and meekly zipped up his fly. I worked three more innings, all without a word from Mr. Harvey.

Point is, though it sometimes may seem otherwise, nobody's perfect in this game. No matter how perfect things look from the outside, always, there is an unzipped fly, or, in my case, a Franklin Stubbs base hit.

Yes, all these years later, he's still *Franklin F@#$%! Stubbs* to me. Though I would become an All-Star in 1992, lead the National League in winning percentage in '92 (.762), lead the NL in walks per nine innings in both '92 and '93 (0.8 both seasons)—and be given the ball by manager Bruce Bochy to start the decisive Game 162 in Dodger Stadium in 1996 and throw seven shutout innings, earning the win that delivered the San Diego Padres the NL West division championship—never was I more on top of my game than on a steamy Friday night in St. Louis in 1990 against the Houston Astros.

It was the night I took a perfect game into the eighth inning, the closest brush with perfection, or even a no-hitter, of my career.

It was August 17, the temperature at first pitch was a sweltering ninety-one degrees and I was coming into the game just as hot. Over my previous nine starts, I had compiled a 1.93 ERA. My season ERA had shrunk by a full three runs, from 5.97 to 2.97, and, by the time I finished a complete-game shutout against Art Howe's Astros, it would zoom all the way down to 2.69.

What nearly ended as a historic night started innocently enough with what I felt was an inauspicious hitter. I had never before faced Houston leadoff man Eric Yelding. I knew little about him, other than this: he could flat-out fly, and I knew that if he got on, he could wreak havoc on the bases. So I went straight to one of my pitching mantras: throw strike one, and get the leadoff hitter out. My first pitch is a fastball down the middle, Yelding shows bunt and pulls back, and plate umpire Bill Hohn raises his fist. Strike one. I come back with a curve, and it travels down and away for ball one.

Next, I throw a fastball down and away for strike two, which opens a variety of options for the next pitch. Ahead in the count, I now have the luxury to go on a fishing expedition, to investigate whether Yelding will expand his strike zone. On a low curve, Yelding does not, and it's 2 and 2. As I stand on the rubber, a quick inventory of the first four pitches reveals . . . Fastball. Curveball. Fastball. Curveball. So while maybe a fastball would seem to be the best pitch right now to Yelding with the count even, I decide to double up on my curve simply to avoid falling into a pattern. One of the worst things a pitcher can do is become predictable, especially in the first inning.

The curve doesn't have much bite and Yelding bounces it toward third where, thankfully, Terry Pendleton is playing even with the bag protecting against a bunt. Do-or-die play right off the bat, he throws to first. Out. Maybe this one leadoff bouncer seems insignificant to the 33,934 filling Busch Stadium on this Friday night, but for me, retiring the leadoff man immediately helps me to relax.

Next up is second baseman Bill Doran. The scouting report says to stay down on him and that you can jam him. Doran is susceptible to inside fastballs. He is known to swing at them, often with the result being a weak ground ball. So as I get set to face him, I repeat to myself: *Strike one. Just throw strike one.* The pitch is a sinker away, left up just a wee bit more than I would have liked, but no matter. Doran rolls over it and sends a weak ground ball to second base. Sweet. This is pitching to contact. To a starting pitcher, one-pitch outs are even more luxurious than a new Bentley.

Now comes yet another hitter I've never faced: Ken Caminiti, Houston's emerging young star. Following Doran's one-pitch at-bat, will Caminiti be swinging early? Or is he more likely to take a pitch or two because of it? What I do know is that the scouting report says Cammy looks for off-speed pitches early in the count. So, now what?

Cat, meet mouse. I'm thinking, *Is Caminiti taking the first pitch no matter what because I just retired Doran on one pitch?* I know Caminiti might be thinking that I'm thinking that Cammy may be taking the first pitch for that reason, so might Cammy be swinging?

Decision on the mound: curveball, down. Caminiti is not swinging. Ball one.

Next pitch, I head straight to my "go-to" spot. Fastball down and away, because with two out and nobody on base, what's the worst that can happen with the pitch? Caminiti slaps a single into left field? Fine, I can live with that, especially because I know that on a 1-and-0 count, the hitter may be looking for something on the inner part of the plate that he can hit hard.

Caminiti offers at the fastball away and pops out to Ozzie Smith at shortstop.

Nearly four years later this very day, on August 18, 1996, I will be a teammate of Caminiti's with the Padres as we play the New York Mets in Monterrey, Mexico, and Cammy is so ill before the game that he's scratched from the lineup before turning in one of the most superhuman performances I've ever seen. Just about everyone else, too. Lying flat on the floor of the manager's office pregame, he took two liters of IV fluids, arose like Lazarus five minutes before game time, munched a Snickers bar and slammed home runs in each of his first two at-bats, singlehandedly staking us to a 4-0 lead en route to an 8-0 win.

Part of the beauty of this game—sometimes, part of its tragedy, too—is that almost always, it is impossible to decipher what's waiting just up ahead for you. And as I get one of my first early glimpses of Caminiti on this hot August night in 1990, it will take a bit before I feel the tug of history—either distant, or immediate.

For the next six innings against the Astros as we build a 5-0 lead, I call up scouting reports in my mental hard drive, spot my fastball, throw an array of crisp curveballs, get-me-over curveballs and even a few of my patented "do drop in" curveballs (brake screechingly slow, thrown in the 68–70 m.p.h. range that hitters sometimes were so eager to dive into that they risked throwing out their backs, not to mention swinging way too early) and more. As I liked to do, some times I reversed course on conventional pitch strategy because I knew hitters often "eliminate" pitches, meaning they don't look for the same pitch you just threw; they'll be looking for something else. So throwing the same pitch you just threw can fool them.

Leading off the second inning is Stubbs, who had just hit home run No. 17 the night before. I know he has pop and I want to get ahead of him, so I start him with a fastball away but miss the strike zone. Now 1 and 0, I know there is a good chance Stubbs is looking for another fastball in this hitter's count, so I cross him up with my first changeup of the game and he dribbles it in front of the plate for an easy out.

Next up is outfielder Glenn Wilson, who, I believe likes the ball up and out over the plate, so I start him with a fastball up and in. Ball one. Since I didn't throw many curveballs to right-handed hitters, I next opt for my "do drop in" curveball, which brings a big swing and a miss. On the mound, I'm thrilled with this development because throwing an off-speed pitch when I'm behind in the count, as I've now done with the past two hitters, is huge. It shows Houston hitters that they cannot sit on a fastball when I am behind in the count. It emphasizes not only my unpredictability, but the fact that I am eminently capable of using it to my advantage.

Following the slo-mo curve, I fire a fastball to induce an easy ground ball to third, bringing up outfielder Tuffy Rhodes. Feeling an early groove, I start him with a curveball for strike one. That's right, no fastball, keep the hitters guessing. Ahead in the count, I throw a fastball that I don't really care whether or not it lands for a strike. The point of this pitch simply is to show the left-handed hitters that I will pitch in. Rhodes fouls it off, so I fire another fastball in because I want to "double up" again and show Rhodes and the other Astros lefties that they cannot eliminate any pitches on this night. Figuring Rhodes is looking for something soft or away, nevertheless, my fastball misses and goes for ball one, then Rhodes fouls off my next pitch, a fastball middle-up, a mistake pitch from me. I missed my location but escaped without Rhodes doing any damage. I collect myself again, breathe, focus and think. I'm ahead in the count 1 and 2 so I have several options with the next pitch. I can go in again with the fastball off the plate for a ball, which would make the count 2 and 2 and open up the plate away, then I can go fastball away, changeup away or curve. Decision: Curveball away following three straight fastballs. It's a good pitch and Rhodes connects, but he whacks it just to the right of second baseman José Oquendo, who moves quickly, backhands the ball and throws Tuffy out by a step.

Two innings, eighteen pitches, six up, six down. And in the bottom of the second, here I come to the plate with one out, runners at the corners and rival starter Bill Gullickson thinking I might squeeze bunt. So the first pitch whizzes by up and in. It's a good thought and something I may do if the situation were reversed. When the pitcher throws a fastball up and in thinking the hitter is bunting, he is hoping the hitter will overcommit to the bunt because it's tremendously difficult to get out of the way of that pitch. And in addition, if a squeeze play is on, it's nearly impossible to stick the bunt on that particular pitch. Usually, it's missed completely and the runner is a dead duck if it is a suicide squeeze and, at worst, it's bunted for a foul ball.

I take it for ball one. And though I'm only hitting .192, I'm swinging pretty well at the time and so my manager, Joe Torre, gives me the green light on the next pitch. I take a good hack and foul it off. Third pitch, the bunt is back on. I square early, giving me the best chance to successfully put the ball in play, and here comes the pitch I am expecting. Curveball. I am expecting a curve because I am thinking Gullickson will go for the strikeout with a runner on third. However, George Kissell, the late and legendary Cardinals coach who was a genius with fundamentals, had a saying that resonated with me: "Track it and whack it." He did a phenomenal job explaining to Cardinals pitchers that it's all about bat angle when you bunt the curve. The change in pitch speed allows the hitter to adjust. I kept my barrel above the ball—you "track it"—bending my knees and not moving the barrel of the bat to get down with the pitch as I move to "whack it." Success. Sacrifice bunt, Oquendo moves to second while Milt Thompson remains at third. And Vince Coleman follows with a single up the middle to score them both.

Exhale, big time. We lead 3-0. I head to the mound to start the third inning with all of my pitches working and, just as importantly, with my mind razor sharp. Everything is in sync at the moment, body, mind, time and place, and what a feeling it is when that happens— which, truth be told, isn't nearly as often as every player would like.

Rich Gedman, a familiar face, steps in to begin the third. I had faced him a couple of times in the 1980s when he was with Boston, and after this night, a year later, in 1991, he will move on to St. Louis to become my teammate. I always enjoyed him because, among other things, we share a common New England heritage, and during one spring game when we were teammates in '91 when he was catching me, he put down one finger to call for a fastball against a right-handed hitter and I shook him off. I wanted to throw a slider but, as I was shaking off the fastball, I thought, *You know, actually, that's a good pitch to throw right now.* So I awaited Geddy's next sign, a curveball, and shook no again. Now I was back to his first call, a fastball, and I wanted to throw it away. I stared in for another sign, he called for a fastball in and I shook again. *C'mon,* I thought, *call for that fastball away.*

Perplexed, Geddy finally put down one last one-finger sign. His middle finger, with strong emphasis as he moved his hand down toward the ground. I started to chuckle so hard I had to put my glove over my face right there on the mound.

Anyway, as Gedman settles in on this night, our radio guy Mike Shannon notes over the KMOX airwaves that the Yankees' Andy Hawkins (of all people) has a no-hitter through six innings in Seattle, and that "our guy has a perfect game thus far." I retire Gedman on a first-pitch fly ball to right field and then, figuring shortstop Rafael Ramírez will be taking after Gedman's expedited at-bat, I fire a first-pitch fastball right down the pipe to Ramírez, who, sure enough, is taking, for strike one. Following a low sinker for ball one, I come back with a curve because I want to put Ramírez off balance and it does exactly that. He's way out in front of it and pops harmlessly to Ozzie Smith at shortstop.

Eight up, eight down, with the pitcher Gullickson up next. Facing the opposing pitcher in the National League is better than a day at Disneyland. In fact, facing the seven-through-nine hitters in the NL is terrific because you can manipulate the lineup. For example, in this situation, I am facing the pitcher with two out and none on and have a great shot at a 1-2-3 inning. If the pitcher leads off an inning, there is a great chance you can follow him by getting the leadoff man out, too. If there is a runner on first base and one out, you simply let the pitcher bunt and obtain an easy out that way, then focus on the top-of-the-order hitters knowing you have an open base and room to work around them, which allows you to focus on making them hit your pitch.

The key is to attack the pitcher, just as I did the other hitters, and not let up. One thing I learned playing in the NL: Hitting is hard! And once you fall behind in the count, it becomes way harder! Memo to pitchers working on the mound: Always remember that. I also know that from the perspective of the guy on the mound, falling behind in the count to the opposing hitter suddenly makes things extremely difficult, because pitchers always are embarrassed when they walk fellow pitchers. And the hot-dog-munching experts in the stands all wonder the same thing, and rightfully so. How in the world did *that* happen?

So I start Gully off with a solid fastball and get ahead in the count 0 and 1. He's a big, strong guy who can put the ball in play, but I notice during that first pitch that he kind of leaned away from the pitch even though it was right down the middle. Hmmm. Was he thinking I was going to go up and in on him after he did it with me while I was bunting? So along those lines, I come in hard again, he fouls it off and, a couple of pitches later, I induce a ground ball to shortstop and our human vacuum cleaner, Ozzie Smith.

In the dugout before the fourth inning, I sit, rest and take it all in. I know things are working. I know I am having a good game. I also know it's really early yet, and I have to keep my focus on obtaining outs and doing what I'm doing. Keep throwing strike one. Get the leadoff hitter out. Okay, here comes the fourth.

Up steps Yelding and, knowing I started him with a fastball to begin the game, I go curveball now. It fools him, gets him out front, and he taps an easy bouncer right back to me. Leadoff man out.

"Hitters get themselves out" is something you hear over and over again during television broadcasts, and it is so true. We pitchers always talk about "just watch batting practice." The BP (batting practice) pitcher is throwing one pitch, the BP fastball, around 50 m.p.h., and so many times hitters *still* don't get hits. They pop these meatballs up, roll over them, miss them. As a pitcher, when you think about this, and then think about adding velocity, location and different types of pitches that you can throw at any time, especially when the pitcher is behind in the count, it makes hitting that much more difficult. The whole "round bat against the round ball and having to hit it square" thing . . . I wanted hitters to hit the ball, but I wanted them to hit *my* pitch and have weak contact.

Next, Doran, who swung at the first pitch his first time up. Thinking he will be aggressive because of this, I start him with a changeup. Strike one, called. Now, I have options again: Fastball in off the plate and then go back away with the next pitch, fastball in and then repeat that with another fastball in, repeat the changeup I just threw . . . Selection: Fastball away. Result: Doran rolls over it and grounds weakly to second. Two out. *Keep focused*, I say to myself.

This brings Caminiti back to the plate and, knowing hitters normally don't swing at a first-pitch curveball, I love it when a pitcher can deliver it with precision and "steal" strike one. This is precisely what I do, followed by a four-seam fastball in for a ball. I want to keep the hitter honest in this spot, and when I did this I always aimed at the belt buckle. It was a good focal point. Pitchers too often get caught in between here, wanting to throw inside but not wanting to hit the batter, and this vacillation often leads to the dreaded fastball right down the middle. Then the pitch gets smoked and the pitcher sees red because how could he miss his location by that much? So my catcher, Todd Zeile, puts down two fingers for the curve, but I think Caminiti probably is sitting on the curve based on the situation and because I haven't given him any pitches to eliminate yet. I want to double up with the fastball, so I shake the curve, come back with a two-seam fastball that runs back over the plate and, bingo, it catches the big third baseman for a called strike three.

Maddux called this strategy "making Xs" because, visually, the hitters see the ball coming in the same location and think it's the same pitch so they "give up" on it . . . and then the ball runs back over the plate. Often, carrying the element of surprise, it causes hitters to jerk their feet back and reflexively lift their arms up as the ball thuds into the mitt—thus "making an X" with the body. Maddux, as you might imagine, became very good at this. And in this key spot in my unforgettable game, it worked beautifully.

Ah, Cammy. In that summer of '96, after I had signed with the Padres as a free agent, he became my son Griffin's favorite player. Then five, Griffin would ask his mother to use mascara to paint a goatee on his face, just like Cammy, and then he would imitate my teammate's batting stances from both sides of the plate while wearing cut-off Padres T-shirts. Whenever I'd take him into the clubhouse, Griffin would run straight to Cammy. One day, Cammy gave him a gold No. 21, which we put on a gold chain for Griffin. As my son got older and we all learned more about Cammy's drug use and addiction, it made him very sad. Cammy was his guy! When he was a teenager, Griffin wrote an essay for entry into St. Paul's School, a high-profile boarding school in Concord, New Hampshire. He also used the essay for his application to Bates College. The essay was all about Cammy, and how people deserve second chances. When Caminiti died in 2004, Griffin cried.

Moments . . .

STARTING THE TOP OF THE FIFTH, my teammates had presented me with a sizeable 5-0 lead which, believe it or not, can be a difficult proposition for a pitcher, especially a young pitcher. First, there's the statistical plateau. Pitchers know that if they can get through the fifth inning with the lead, they qualify for a win. That right there becomes a distraction because pitchers too often start thinking about the win instead of about simply making their next pitch. They get too far ahead of themselves, which causes a loss of focus, a very public disintegration and an early exit from the game. I know. I went through this plenty myself as a young pitcher. With time, I trained myself to lock in, zero in on pitching seven or eight innings every outing and to believe that the fifth inning was simply another inning, same as the first, second or fourth.

I started the leadoff man, Stubbs, with a fastball away for a called strike, then dropped in a curveball for another called strike. Cooking with gas, as they say. I could do anything I wanted. Now, ahead 0 and 2 in the count, I've got practically more options than I can count. I've gone hard, then slow. Stubbs cannot have any idea what I will throw next. Probably, though, he suspects it will not be a strike. Why wouldn't I try to tempt him to chase? I know that, depending on what this pitch is, he's probably going to guess at the second pitch I throw from this point as well. I will try to twist him like a mall pretzel, so I tease him with a curveball even slower than the one I just threw, in the dirt, while planning to follow that up either with a fastball or with a changeup that, after a couple of curves, will *look* like the fastball he is anticipating and hopefully produce very soft contact.

Except, the curveball I throw? I baby it while attempting to throw it even slower than the preceding curve and, as a result, it stays high. It is my thirty-ninth pitch, and it is the first one of the evening that I would call a "noncompetitive pitch," meaning it does absolutely nothing to enhance the last pitch in any way, nor does it do anything to set up my next pitch. The reason I change speeds on my curveball is to mess with the hitters' timing. Most likely, hitters will be out in front of my curve, and if I can slow it down from there, they will swing even farther out in front of it. I used to employ this tactic with Pudge Rodríguez all the time because he would forever be yanking my curveballs down the third-base line foul with no chance of keeping the ball fair. And more often than not, he swung wildly and missed it altogether. Career, he was 3 for 11 against me with three strikeouts.

Zeile signals fastball in on the 1 and 2 pitch to Stubbs but I shake him off a couple of times. The fastball in is a good pitch, but it also follows a pattern I've been showing to hitters. As the game moves into the middle innings, I feel like I've showed the fastball in enough to make Houston hitters aware of it, and once they're aware of it, it leaves the outside part of the plate wide open. Zeile then calls for a curve, which I shake again because I've just thrown two of them. So we settle on a pitch I haven't thrown yet, a backdoor slider. I want to make it look like a fastball away, which the hitter would give up on and maybe get taken to the cleaners with a called third strike. But the pitch runs back over the plate. Stubbs is out in front of it quite a bit and flies to right field. I may have gotten a bit lucky right here. I'll take it.

Next I get Wilson with a one-pitch curveball, then induce an easy fly ball from Rhodes, the rookie, and I'm out of the fifth after only eight pitches—and only forty-three for the night.

In the bottom of the fifth, we go down 1-2-3 and I don't mind this a bit. With a five-run lead, we're in good shape. And on the mound, I am in a good rhythm so a quick inning gets me back out there without much of a wait.

My rhythm is kept intact when Gedman swings at my first pitch of the sixth and pops it up to left field, and Ramírez swings at my second pitch and rolls a grounder to third base. Three pitches, two outs, the buzz in Busch Stadium beginning to grow as things become more serious by the batter. In the stands, unbeknownst to me, Laura was fighting the heat by drinking a large lemonade and, after holding off the urge to go to the bathroom for a long while because she did not want to leave her seat and jinx me, she finally could wait no longer and made a quick exit to the ladies' room.

Next, Howe sends Dave Rohde to the plate to bat for pitcher Dan Schatzeder. Good pinch hitters hunt first-pitch fastballs, so I start Rohde off with a curveball for a strike followed by a fastball up-and-in that catches him in a check swing. Foul ball, 0 and 2. I throw two more fastballs, ball one and another foul ball, then another one that is up. After three consecutive fastballs, all up, I want to change Rohde's eye level with something down in the zone. So I go curve, Rohde chops down at it and misses, and the Cardinals and I are perfect through six. Much to the relief of my wife, now back from the restroom for the game's final stages.

As we begin the seventh, the entire stadium is aware of the situation. In the field, I can sense that some of the position players behind me are becoming a little bit more tense. Nobody wants to be the guy to mess up a perfect game.

Yelding leads off, and I own the strike zone. First pitch, fastball away, called strike. Second pitch, curveball down, called strike. Preparation is meeting opportunity, time is meeting place, momentum is meeting my right arm. I throw a cutter away for a ball, then come back with a curveball and Yelding is out in front of it. Ground ball to third, one out.

Next up, I drop in a first-pitch curveball for a strike to Doran, work him to 1 and 2 and then drop the hammer with another curveball for a called strike three. Then Cammy, who is sitting on a first-pitch curveball but gets too far under it and flies to right field.

"Tewks! Tewks! Tewks!"

As I jog off the mound, jersey soaked through with sweat, water droplets beading the brim of my cap, I can feel (and hear) the excitement crackling through the Friday-night Busch Stadium crowd on this summer's evening. The fans have moved to high alert, having arrived at the ballpark hoping for a Cardinals win but now that's been upgraded big time as they sense history and serenade me back to the dugout. "Tewks! Tewks! Tewks!" For the first time all evening, I am beginning to feel something else in my veins: pressure. A perfect game? Me? A couple of teammates give me an "Attaboy!" but as I reach the dugout, nobody sits near me. I want another quick inning now. I do not want to sit here and think about this for very long. Yogi's "baseball is 90 percent mental and the other half is physical"? Yep, this night is an excellent interpretation of that.

In the dugout, the only person to come near me is Brad, our trainer, who offers "the towel." It is a white towel that has been soaking in ammonia water and ice since the start of the game. Players loved the towel, especially on hot, humid St. Louis nights. It cooled you down, and inhaling ammonia seemed to clear your mind. Brad drapes the towel over my face, and it is oh so reinvigorating. I take a long inhale, pulling the ammonia smell through my nostrils. My head feels the kick. I lean forward and Brad drapes the towel over the nape of my neck and holds it there for a few seconds more before leaving me to prepare for what is coming.

Twenty-one hitters up, twenty-one hitters down. I have not had a three-ball count yet. I've had only three two-ball counts. Six Astros, knowing I am pumping strikes, have swung at the first pitch. So now, the chess match *really* begins. What do I throw to the leadoff hitter, Stubbs, to start the eighth? The heavy lifting now is in working to slow down my thoughts, which are firing through my mind like a succession of racquetballs bounding off a wall. I am starting to *think* about my pitch selections rather than go by feel and instinct. I find myself *trying* to be perfect. What do I throw Stubbs? I pace the dugout and seek out Zeile. I want to know what his thoughts are. We decide to go with my strength, fastball away, and see what happens. I think, *If this is going to end, please let it end this inning, not in the ninth.*

By baseball standards as that eighth inning started, I was perfect.

But by so many other measures, given that thoughts were outpacing my ability to process them and I wasn't even sure that I wouldn't be relieved if my bid ended, I was far from it.

"Tewks! Tewks! Tewks!"

Lots of crazy stuff is flitting through my mind. Foremost among the thoughts is that finally, I am establishing myself deeper and deeper in the major leagues with each pitch. Five days earlier, I had thrown a complete-game shutout at Pittsburgh's Three Rivers Stadium. Now here I am, on the brink of a second consecutive shutout, with a perfect game a very real possibility. By evening's end, I would be 8-3 and, I hoped, every victory would further cement my spot on the team for a good, long time. Now, what do I throw Stubbs?

Looking back today, he continues to consistently roll through my thoughts as *Franklin F@#$%! Stubbs*, and I can't help but smile at that. Out we went to begin the eighth inning, and out came the strategy that Zeile and I had agreed to deploy. My strength, fastball away, first pitch. Stubbs doesn't hit it well, but well enough. The ball heads toward left field, and we have just moved left-fielder Coleman to shade toward center as the lefty Stubbs had pulled everything prior to that. The ball lands where Coleman isn't, Stubbs makes it to second base and my quest for perfection is finished.

I remember straddling the pitching rubber and exhaling. Part of me was relieved that it was over. At the same time, part of me wondered whether I had thrown the right pitch. And then, my mind shifted back toward the next goal. Perfect game over, I could still secure my second consecutive shutout.

In the dugout after the eighth inning, I accepted consolation from my teammates, who were hoping that together we could make this a night for the ages. I chat with my catcher, who says it was "a good pitch." I still second-guess my pitch selection and location. And I am not happy with my thought process, for wanting the pressure to end, even in some small way, instead of full-on going for it.

In the moment, I am able to maintain my equilibrium enough to mow through the next three hitters, strand Stubbs and then pitch a 1-2-3 ninth. In the end, I faced just twenty-eight batters, one over the minimum, surrendering just one hit, striking out three and throwing only seventy-nine pitches (58 for strikes). I feel like I have established myself in the majors, once and for all, with consecutive complete-game shutouts. Overall, I am really happy and not overly concerned with what could have been.

However, that fall when we return home, it all changes. As the chill of another New England autumn settles in, I'm cleaning out our garage one day and daydreaming about what might have been on that special night in St. Louis in the summer's heat. Could I have done anything differently? Did I throw the right pitch? What if I had thrown a curve? Would I have gotten the next hitter? Had my thoughts affected my performance? Did I set myself up for the near miss with my thinking? How would I have handled the ninth inning if I *had* gotten through the eighth still perfect?

Yes, perfect by baseball standards . . . but imperfect by others.

As I stood there in the garage, I realized I had to put things in perspective. I had to find some way to feel good about having pitched a one-hit, complete-game shutout, not like I had failed in trying to attain perfection. I was twenty-nine years old, just a couple of years beyond shoulder surgery, and a night that started with me working to make another pitch to stay in the rotation ended with me suddenly thinking of and obsessing over something else.

IT HAS BEEN many years since that game, yet there still are times, especially when someone today comes so close to throwing a perfect game—like Washington's Max Scherzer, who in 2015 lost a bid with two outs in the ninth when he hit a batter with a pitch—that I think about what might have been on that steamy August night in the Gateway City. I'm kinder to myself now, but on that autumn day in my garage, my reevaluation and recollection sure did not make me feel good. Instead, I felt empty and remorseful, like I had failed. I didn't understand it in that moment, but I've since learned that this type of thinking is distorted, unhealthy and unnecessary.

Today, one of the most common self-descriptions I hear from players is that they consider themselves to be "perfectionists." Many acknowledge that they are overly critical of their own performances, as if that's a good thing, an admirable trait. My answer to them is clear. There is a difference between those who strive for perfection versus those who simply will not settle for anything less.

Harvey Dorfman, an early mentor to athletes a couple of decades ago and the author of the book *The Mental Game of Baseball: A Guide to Peak Performance*, when discussing perfection would ask the player: "Do you know anyone who is perfect?" The player, of course, would say no. So Harvey would respond: "So then what makes you think you'll be the first one to be perfect?" He also used to advise players this about perfection: "When you return to your hotel room after a game, turn on the water in the bathtub, let it fill about four inches, and then step in. If your feet don't touch the tub, *then* you can try to be perfect."

Often, these types of standards are influenced by parents or coaches who demand perfection, coming at things from the viewpoint that no matter what you do, you can always do better, that one shouldn't "settle" for anything less than a perfect performance.

A minor league player once told me a story of the time he went 3 for 4 at the plate with two RBIs and then phoned his dad to share his accomplishment. The player thought his father would be excited, yet, instead, Dad chided him for making an out, his only out, with the bases loaded. This type of thinking is not exclusive to athletes, either. I recall my daughter once telling me that one of her high school teammates was grounded by her mother because she didn't get a 100 percent on a biology exam. The slacker got "only" a 97!

There is a key difference between those who strive for perfection and those who refuse to accept anything less. Striving for perfection focuses on the execution of a particular skill, working to do it the best you possibly can, like a hitter looking to make solid contact with the baseball. It's perfectly healthy, as people maintain confidence in their performance by focusing on what they can control. These people exhibit the ability to cope with the challenges of performance and the adjustments that need to be made. They are able to do this in large part because they realize the results are out of their control. If something doesn't go well, they are able to let it go and look ahead to the next task facing them. They do not equate their self-image with the achievement of perfection which, as we know, is an impossibility.

Conversely, those who are obsessed with perfection focus too much on the results and, consequently, have a distorted view of success and consider anything short of it as a failure. Perfectionism takes away from enjoyment, not only in a particular performance but in life in general. Perfectionists establish a pattern of beliefs that involves setting unrealistic goals and expectations, and standards that are impossible to meet. The result? They are guaranteed to never be good enough, and it sets them up for one frustration after another.

Perfectionists tend to have low self-confidence, making it difficult for them to cope when things don't go as expected. And in search of gaining confidence, they practice more and more, which increases the risk of burnout. The constant striving for perfection creates high levels of anxiety, they worry more about what others think of them and they focus more on their failures than on their successes. Also, they tend to make excuses for poor performances because they are unable to accept their mistakes.

The rub is, in order to become an elite athlete, a person must highly develop his or her skills through exhaustive repetition while attempting to get as close as possible to, yes, perfection. This is why most athletes tend to be perfectionists. The tipping point, though, is when it reaches the stage of "I *have* to be perfect."

As I work with players today, one of the things I do is try to help them strive for perfection while illustrating the negative consequences that *having* to be perfect can bring. It is not an easy line to straddle, especially in a bright-spotlight, heavy-pressure, big-dollar sport in which far more dreams are crushed than are cashed in. I didn't—*couldn't*—recognize that difference early in my career, either. But that near-perfect night against the Astros and its aftermath led me to thinking, studying and observing. And as I moved through the rest of my career in St. Louis, Texas, San Diego and Minnesota, I began constructing a mindset that was more healthy and less distorted.

7

Joe Torre and the Permission to Succeed

Joe Torre was as close to a mental skills coach as there was in 1991, and as he guided those New York Yankees teams to one World Series victory after another a few years later, his genius at this level was on the October stage for all to see. For me, I saw it up close, in his St. Louis manager's office a couple of seasons after Ted Simmons's honesty sent me into overdrive, again, with my mental imagery, and helped launch my career.

Take one of this scene comes at old (and now imploded) Veterans Stadium in Philadelphia on Sunday, May 9, 1993. I'm on the mound in the eighth inning, two out, we're leading 5-2 and, as they say in the South, I should be sitting in tall cotton right about now, right? Except, butter my butt and call me a biscuit, Darren Daulton strokes a single and Wes Chamberlain follows by lacing a double. Second and third, two out, here comes Torre out of the dugout.

Now, a couple of things right here. These 1993 Phillies were phearsome. Yes, that's right. *Phearsome*. Lineup so strong with Daulton, Lenny Dykstra, Dave Hollins, John Kruk, Mariano Duncan and the rest that they could knock the spelling right out of you and make you lose an f right then and there. Before you knew it, you would be standing on the mound thinking, "What the *f*? And, where did the *f* go, anyway?" This would be one of those afternoons.

Later that season, the Phillies would run the table all the way to Game 6 of the World Series, where they would be vanquished by Rickey Henderson, Paul Molitor, Roberto Alomar, Joe Carter and the rest of the Toronto Blue Jays. On this May afternoon, though, they were my problem. And as Torre walked toward me on the mound, I thought the handwriting on the wall read that my day was done. Even though this was Torre's third full season managing the Cardinals, I was still conditioned to the way his predecessor, Hall of Famer Whitey Herzog, ran things. Among Whitey's strengths was his deft handling of the bullpen; he really did a beautiful job with that. And with big Lee Arthur Smith ensconced there to close games, I essentially had become trained to work six or seven innings before being lifted.

Trained, that is, in multiple ways. Many times performance matches self-image, and perhaps with all of those calls to the bullpen for Smith, I may have been performing to match my own self-image. And once that is ingrained, it can be extremely difficult to expand the limitations you perhaps unwittingly place on yourself. Even though I had made the All-Star team the year before, in a way in early '93, I was reverting back to the "striving to get to The Show and stay there" kid, as opposed to the accomplished and confident pitcher the manager believed in. Sometimes, becoming more than a six- or seven-inning pitcher is not just about physical stamina. And in this instance, looking back, I think I needed to push myself to make the mental jump to become that next-level MLB pitcher. I would go on to win seventeen games in '93, and this was a turning point.

So . . . as Torre approaches the mound in the eighth inning, I believe in my mind that I am out of the game. But the purpose of this visit from Torre is to read my body language, not necessarily to remove me.

The problem: My body language at the moment, triggered by my mental reaction, screams "Done!"

Seeing it, Torre executes that long-honored National League strategic move and double-switches me out of the game. Smith enters, walks the first batter he faces, Milt Thompson, to load the bases. Then, he surrenders a first-pitch grand slam to Duncan. Phillies win, 6-5, and the flight home is not a happy one. I knew I had given in, and I hated myself for it.

Cut to take two of this scene, following a Monday off day, before Tuesday's home-stand opener against the New York Mets in St. Louis. Not long after I arrive at the ballpark, eager to talk with my manager about what had happened last time out and what I was thinking, Torre beats me to the punch and summons me into his office. Turns out, he has the same reaction as me. We need to talk.

"Do you know why I took you out of the game Sunday?" Torre asks.

I respond: "Because I didn't say anything to keep myself in the game."

Torre agrees.

"Tweksie [for some reason, instead of calling me Tewks like everybody else, Torre called me Tweksie in those days], you may not have the same stuff as a Tom Glavine or Greg Maddux, but I believe in you. You can pitch, and win, at this level."

With those words, my resolve was strengthened. What I needed to do was to continue to believe in myself as much as my manager believed in me.

This manager's approach was on the opposite end of the spectrum from Lou Piniella's demand of "What the hell are you doing?" Where Lou brought the vinegar, Joe provided sugar. Though we all play the same game and share the same goals, the always-changing blend of personalities, characters, temperaments and road maps to travel from point A to point B are entirely different. Some cultures foster confidence, teamwork and positive outlooks. Others breed anxiety, worry and conditions in which it is almost impossible for a player to consistently perform at peak ability. There is no one size fits all.

Always, Piniella, one of the game's great characters, has been known for his short fuse, lovable (much of the time) impatience and volcanic temper. Clearly, as both a player and as a manager, it did not impede him. After our time together with the Yankees, he managed the 1990 Cincinnati Reds to a stunning World Series upset victory over the powerful Oakland Athletics, and he guided the Seattle Mariners to some great seasons after that, including their 116-win summer in 2001. What he did worked for a lot of people. But while few things have been indisputable throughout the more than one hundred years of history of this game, this one is. Different players bring different psyches, just like the children in your family or the coworkers in your office. Try to handle every one of them the same and chances are you're going to lose some along the way. Humorous and clever as it was, the old line about the legendary Green Bay Packers coach Vince Lombardi treating all of his players the same, like dogs . . . well, that's Stone Age stuff in today's games, whatever the sport.

As old school as Torre is in so many ways, even way back then he was enlightened in the way he treated players, coaxing their best efforts through confidence-boosting conversations and relationships. From that discussion in his office, I emerged with a newfound confidence that would propel me through another half decade of pitching in St. Louis, Texas, San Diego and Minnesota. I would also emerge with a couple of terms that I employ today as I build and nurture relationships with the modern player: "permission to be successful" and "thoughts become things."

Torre's message to me, essentially, was that I had to give myself permission to succeed. My term, not his. His mind was open when he walked to the mound in Philadelphia that afternoon. All the way, he intended to base his decision on what he saw from me. I was the one who needed a different thought process. I was the one who, instead of expecting to get hooked, needed to give myself permission to succeed so that I would have what I needed to continue pushing forward. I had pitching coaches who believed in me as a young pitcher. Mark Connor, Sammy Ellis and Joe Coleman, to name three. Especially Coleman—I don't want to minimize his impact. It was enormous. But it was Torre who had the most impact, for a very clear reason. He was the manager. There are many pitching coaches along the way with whom you click, and maybe one or two become indispensable, like Coleman with me. But . . . if the manager doesn't like you or trust you, you don't pitch. Plain and simple.

Having the manager's "blessing," so to speak, was like getting it from your dad, not your uncle or grandpa. For me, the skipper was Piniella in New York. And Don Zimmer in Chicago—and I stunk there, so I know he didn't like me. Herzog didn't call me up in 1989 because he didn't feel I had the stuff, so he went with a four-man rotation until September.

Then Torre came along.

"We talked quite a bit because he always wanted to know things," Torre says today. "He asked a lot of questions and wanted to know chapter and verse about thought process and things like that. I do remember going out to the mound. A lot of times when managers go to the mound, they're the one who is taking the pitcher out. I remember in my first managing job with the Mets going out to the mound and I was going to talk with Jerry Koosman. Jerry handed me the ball. Well, that solved that problem.

"It was very similar. Tewksie didn't hand me the ball but he didn't say anything that would encourage me to leave him in. To me, once you take yourself out of the game mentally, you can't crank it back up again emotionally. After that incident with Koosman, I made up my mind that if I had to go talk to a pitcher, I jogged out, and if I was taking him out, I walked out. After the Koosman incident I started doing that, to at least give the pitcher a heads-up that he doesn't *have* to hand me the ball."

Some managers have a preconceived prejudice against pitchers who do not possess overpowering stuff. Torre, more patient, did not. In fact, when he was still managing, he was discussing in this vein a particular left-hander with Hall of Famer Sandy Koufax, and Koufax told him: "It's not what you throw, but where you throw it."

"That taught me a lot because it's so true," Torre says. "As a player myself, you could look for a fastball and if the fastball was put in the right spot to where you could not hit it, or to where you couldn't do much with it, it would negate the fact that you knew what was coming. Tewksie threw not only in and out but up and down. He was an artist.

"When somebody knows their ability, you have a better chance to sharpen what you do."

Make no mistake that thoughts quickly can become things, and that last thought is one you can exhibit for evidence. If a pitcher thinks along the lines of "don't walk this guy," "that pitch was a strike," "the ump screwed me" or "I can't give up any runs" and allows that thought any oxygen at all, then it quickly can evolve into a real thing. Suddenly when you're on the mound, instead of giving

100 percent of your focus and energy to your next pitch and the execution of it, which is where your mind should be, your thoughts are becoming corroded with a negative feeling and emotion. That's the opposite of confidence. That is a wing and a prayer, with a healthy side of what we commonly know as fear.

I can identify it so readily today to the players I try to help because there were times in my career when I lived it. And on every one of those occasions, I had to face it and figure out a path around it; otherwise, my career would have been short-circuited like so many others.

The thing that is both odd and instructive when it comes to that meeting with Torre in 1993 is that I was coming off of a career year. In 1992, I went 16-5 with a 2.16 ERA for the Cardinals, led the National League with a .762 winning percentage and finished third in the NL Cy Young voting. My 0.77 walks-per-nine-innings rate was the lowest in the majors since Cincinnati's Red Lucas in 1933 (0.74), and not only that, only three other pitchers in the entire *century* posted a walks rate so low: the Pittsburgh Pirates' Babe Adams (0.62 in 1920), Hall of Famer Christy Mathewson (0.62 in 1913 and 0.66 in 1914) and Hall of Famer Cy Young himself (0.69 in 1904). And not only was I named to the All-Star team, but NL manager Bobby Cox called on me to start the fifth inning of the game on July 14, 1992, in San Diego's Jack Murphy Stadium. It was one of the crowning moments of my career, yet also brought with it another example of thoughts becoming things.

For the better part of three months, to start the 1992 season, I was locked in physically and mentally, and my performance on the mound was as consistent as it ever would be in my thirteen years in the majors. I was 9-3 with a 1.87 ERA at the break and standing tall. My confidence was peaking. Everything was scripted from the time one game ended until my next start five days later. I knew when and how much I would run, lift weights and throw. I studied my next opponent's tendencies, strengths and weaknesses. I visualized, and my visions came true. I was in control of any situation I was presented with and felt I could beat anyone I faced.

Though some uncertainties began churning through my mind as my wife, my young son (Griffin was two at the time) and I hopped into a limousine for the short ride from Los Angeles to San Diego following the Sunday series-finale in Dodger Stadium leading into the All-Star break, by game time on Tuesday those uncertainties and the feeling of great expectations had subsided. My mind was at rest and my confidence had returned.

At the same time, I knew this experience was going to be totally different. Accustomed to starting, of course, I would be coming out of the bullpen. Tom Glavine had earned the honor of starting, and that meant my pregame preparation would have to be different. Additionally, as All-Stars, we would have the spotlight to ourselves on this Tuesday night, and I knew what that meant. Not only would my wife and son be in the stands, but the entire country would be watching, especially my family and friends back home in New Hampshire. For one night, I would be among greatness. I would be one of *them*, the best in the game. I desperately wanted to pitch well, to show everyone I truly did belong.

On the outside, I may have looked calm and confident. But on the inside, wow. No matter how much you train yourself mentally, when the stakes are this high and the honor this magnificent, the emotions, anxiety and excitement attach themselves to your stomach like an anchor keeping a boat in the harbor. The pregame introductions alone were something I'll never forget. There I was, being introduced right alongside fourteen future Hall of Famers: Glavine, Maddux, John Smoltz, Ozzie Smith, Tony Gwynn, Sandberg, Craig Biggio, Kirby Puckett, Wade Boggs, Roberto Alomar, Cal Ripken Jr., Paul Molitor, Ken Griffey Jr., and Dennis Eckersley.

As I heard my name echo throughout Jack Murphy Stadium, ricocheting around the concourses like a batting-practice home run ball through an empty section of seats, I took a step forward toward the cameraman kneeling in front of me. I tipped my cap and gazed toward the grandstand, to the seating section reserved for players' families and guests. I was looking for Laura and Griffin, and my heart sank because I couldn't find them. Again, my mind began racing. Was something wrong? The rest of the introductions and pageantry were a blur. Concern regarding my family was distracting me from enjoying the moment. I assured myself that everything was fine, that there must be a good reason as to why I couldn't see them in the stands.

Turns out, there was. What I didn't know at the time was that the family bus's entrance into the stadium parking lot had been delayed by the motorcades of President George H. W. Bush and Carlos Salinas de Gortari, president of Mexico, who were attending the game. Once again, thoughts become things. Things that rattle around in your mind like those monsters under the bed when you are a kid. Get them out of here!

The plan was for Glavine to work the first two innings, followed by Maddux or David Cone and, after that, the rest of us pitchers were on call, not knowing when our opportunities might arise. As a starting pitcher, everything is planned: the day you are going to pitch, the time you get up, the time you eat, when you go to the ballpark, when you warm up and for how long. You are in control of your preparation. Whenever I had worked in relief in the past, it always had increased my performance anxiety. And now, I would be asked to pitch out of the pen . . . in an All-Star Game! My anxiety climbed to new heights.

Then, *boom!* Glavine got peppered for nine singles and five runs in the first two innings, Maddux was summoned in relief in the second and everything suddenly was even more off-kilter. The bullpen phone rang in the middle of the fourth, they told me I had the fifth and, finally able to size up the situation, knowing who I likely would be facing, I actually began to settle down again.

It's showtime! I thought as the fourth inning ended, a spike of adrenaline surging through my body as I took the field to start the fifth. Catcher Darren Daulton met me at the mound to go over which signs we would use and then I quietly repeated my pitching mantra to myself: *Strike one, get the leadoff hitter out.* Then I promptly threw two straight balls to Joe Carter, who already had two hits and one RBI in the game. Slowly, I drew a deep breath—*breathe, breathe, breathe*—and went back to my self-talk. *Just like on the side*, I reminded myself, same thing I had told myself all season whenever I fell behind in the count. Refocused, reminded to pitch free and easy, I fired a fastball away and induced a harmless pop fly to second base.

Up next, Mark McGwire, who came into the game leading the majors with twenty-eight homers. I jumped ahead by throwing a curveball for a called strike, fell to even in the count with a slider away for a ball, then got another pop fly to second on a fastball away. So far, so good. Now, Ripken. I reminded myself, *Bear down*, then threw a fastball away for a called strike, followed by a fastball away for ball one. Ripken fouled off the next pitch—I remember thinking, *Oh, I might have gotten away with one there.* I liked to repeat pitches, so I went with another inside fastball, a pitch Ripken fouled straight down so hard it bounced straight up and hit him in the shoulder. Except, plate ump Doug Harvey, "God," who thought he saw all and knew all, didn't see the ball hit Ripken's shoulder and didn't ask for help. Daulton alertly picked it up and tagged out Ripken, and I had a nifty 1-2-3 inning and ten pitches. Whew.

As I walked off the mound, I felt a great sense of relief wash over me. I was thirty-one years old, had overcome surgeries, a release, several demotions and now here I was in the midst of the best season of my career. I had retired every batter I faced in an All-Star Game.

I could put my mind at rest. Now, I could relax and enjoy the rest of the evening.

When I saw Bobby Cox walking my way in the dugout, I assumed he was coming over to congratulate me on my outing. Which he definitely was, except, following "Hey, nice job!" he had more to say. "You feeling okay?" he asked.

You feeling okay? This is a question managers often ask of pitchers, and it is the one that most pitchers hate the most. Ask a pitcher how he feels, the majority of the time the pitcher will lie. Fine. Great. I think the majority of pitchers would prefer that the manager simply make the call. Leave me in or take me out. But be decisive.

So, I lied. "I'm fine," I told Cox.

He nodded at the answer he expected to hear.

"Good," he said. "We're going to keep you in for one more."

My heart sank. The joyous feelings of success and contentment that had filled my body just moments earlier immediately started to drain. I hadn't expected this. It's not often that a pitcher enters an All-Star Game in relief and pitches more than one inning. I had shut down mentally as soon as I'd gotten that third out to end the fifth. When a pitcher shuts down, it is really difficult to get the mind ramped up to compete again. But what was I supposed to say? "No, Bobby, I don't want to pitch another inning in an All-Star Game"? I mean, I had thrown only ten pitches so I was fine physically. But mentally, I was not.

So I sat there in the dugout, waiting for the inning to end so I could go back out there and, once again, I was filled with anticipation. Only this time the excitement I felt earlier was replaced by trepidation and fear of failure. I tried to battle these negative thoughts as best I could, but it was like trying to put a cork back into a champagne bottle. As I took off my warm-up jacket after we went down 1-2-3 in the fifth, my inner voice echoed: *Okay, don't screw this up.* I shook my head, as if that might shake the negativity from my mind.

I jogged to the mound, threw my warm-ups, then stepped off behind the mound to focus. *Nice and easy,* I told myself. *Just get the leadoff man out.* Same mantra I used last inning. Only now, it felt like a statement of hope, not conviction.

Ken Griffey Jr. led off the fifth. His dad was a key member of Cincinnati's "Big Red Machine" in the 1970s and was a teammate of mine in New York when I was a rookie with the Yankees in 1986. In fact, he was the left-fielder in my first major league start, with Hall of Famer Rickey Henderson in center field and Hall of Famer Dave Winfield in right field. "Junior," as everyone knew Griffey's son back then, was a powerful left-hander with few weaknesses who would join Henderson and Winfield in Cooperstown when he was finished playing. I felt the best way to retire him was to mix up my pitches and work to keep him off balance. So I threw a first-pitch curveball, which went for ball one. Thinking that Griffey now would be sitting on a fastball, I tried to throw one down and away that he might roll over to the right side of the infield. Instead, the pitch ran back to the middle of the plate and Griffey smashed a double into the right-field gap.

Ah damn, I said to myself. *Here we go.* Thoughts of doubt and fear, which had started in the dugout in the seconds after Cox informed me he wanted one more inning, started to gain momentum. To the 59,372 fans in Jack Murphy Stadium and the millions watching on television, Griffey's gapper was just a double. But to me, it represented trouble.

Next up was Roberto Alomar, a switch-hitter, which meant I would see him from the left side of the plate, too. Robby was a lot like Griffey, minus the power. I started him with a fastball, he fouled it back, I repeated with another fastball, and Alomar was out in front of the pitch and grounded to first. Griffey advanced to third, but I had gotten a much-needed out, so I took a deep breath and moved forward.

With Brady Anderson, another lefty who followed Alomar, my entire focus was on recording an out, even if it meant Griffey scored. I just wanted to prevent a big inning. But because I was uncomfortable with my curve after the poor one I had thrown Griffey, I decided to start Anderson with a fastball away and the pitch was low. I came back with another fastball, this one down and away, and Anderson rolled over it, punched a routine ground ball to first and I had my second out.

Countering my nervousness and fear was the "2" on the scoreboard under "Outs." *All right*, I told myself. *I am one pitch away from getting out of this*. When I saw Cleveland's young, switch-hitting second baseman, Carlos Baerga, coming to the plate, I knew he was an aggressive hitter and figured he would swing early. Since I had started the two previous hitters with fastballs, I felt I needed to try something different. Though I wasn't 100 percent confident with my curveball, I knew it was the right pitch to throw.

Problem: My lack of true conviction with the execution of throwing the pitch resulted in a poorly thrown pitch, which stayed up high for ball one. Now, it might have been a good time to double up with the curve but I went fastball, which Carlos swung at and missed, and the count was 1 and 1. Now, options. I could go back to the curveball or throw another fastball as long as I kept it down in the zone. My choice was fastball, but like that earlier heater to Griffey, it stayed up in the zone—right in Baerga's wheelhouse. He whacked it to left-center, scoring Griffey.

What I should have seen as no big deal—one run in, man on second but two outs—suddenly I perceived as a wildfire threatening to rage out of control. I needed to flee. My body started to tense up, my chest felt tight, my mind became utterly distracted. Robin Ventura was next and I tried to change my approach again by starting him with a backdoor slider. He spit at it, watching the pitch stay off the plate for ball one. I evened the count by throwing my first changeup of the game for a called strike and, thinking Ventura would eliminate the changeup as a pitch to look for, I threw another but it missed down in the zone. Now, with the count 2 and 1, I opted for a fastball in. Bad idea. Trying to sneak a fastball by the smooth, deadly quick Ventura was like trying to sneak a T-bone past a black Labrador. Robin smashed a hard liner down the line, past first baseman Fred McGriff, for the third double of the inning, scoring Baerga.

What I feared happening was happening. A thousand thoughts were flooding my mind. I knew I should have pitched only one inning. I should have thrown a changeup there. I can't believe this is happening on national TV. I felt exposed and embarrassed. I wanted this inning to end in the worst way.

When power-hitting outfielder Rubén Sierra stepped to the plate, I was hoping he would just hit the ball at someone and end this bad dream. I got ahead of him with a changeup for a strike, but missed wide with a fastball away on the next pitch. I gazed in at Sierra, and he looked way too comfortable at the plate. It's amazing how hitters gain momentum when their lineup strings a few hits together. As they come to the plate, it's as if each of them, one by one, smells blood. They look toward the mound knowing the prey is wounded and sense it is time to go for the kill.

I was the prey now, and I knew it.

My mind was drowning in "don'ts." I don't have a feel for my curveball, so I can't throw that. I don't really have command of my fastball today, either. What the hell should I throw now? Working under the theory that desperate times call for desperate measures, I decided to try to trick Rubén with a changeup. The pitch did trick him, but not enough. He swung and was out in front of the pitch, so much so that his top hand came off the bat before it connected with the ball. But, it was solid contact nonetheless. It landed for a two-run, one-handed home run.

In my peripheral vision, I could see that someone was (mercifully?) warming up in the bullpen, as Travis Fryman, the inning's seventh hitter, walked to the plate. I was numb. I felt hopeless. My All-Star dream had become a nightmare. *This can't be real. What the hell just happened?*

I thought my first two pitches were strikes, but Harvey called them balls. More unwelcome thoughts. You've gotta be kidding me, Doug! Give me a break. I never walk anyone. I am out here getting crushed and you're going to squeeze me now? I was so distracted by the injustice of it all that my next two pitches were not within two zip codes of the strike zone, and I issued Fryman a four-pitch walk.

I knew that would be it for me, and as Cox walked to the mound, I felt relief. But, it was a far different breed of relief from what I'd experienced as I walked off the mound the inning before. Which, by the way, seemed like hours ago. I had been one out away from pitching two scoreless innings in the All-Star Game, but it had all unraveled. Cox approached and gently said, "Well, Tewks, gotta make a move here." I didn't say a word. I just handed him the ball.

As I analyzed all of this over the next few years, I came to a few conclusions. I should have done my job, staying locked in, until I was told I was finished for the night. That almost certainly would have allowed me to keep my mental edge. I should have controlled my thoughts better, keeping my inner dialogue positive and more focused on the task at hand. I should have not personalized what happened to "me." That alone created and heaped on more anxiety and stress. And I should have viewed things in smaller, consumable bites. *Make your next pitch, and keep blinders on to everything else.*

My sixth-inning troubles aside, you would think that the All-Star invitation in general, my fifth-inning success and my overall dominance in 1992 (again, I led the NL with a .762 winning percentage and finished third in Cy Young voting!) would have propelled me to the point in May 1993 that, when Torre came to visit me on the mound, I would have greeted him with far more confidence and chutzpah than I did. But this is a game that excels at knocking players off balance when they least expect it. I had battled my entire career for a place in the major leagues, to believe that I belonged in the majors, and to some degree that battle is never finished, no matter how many innings you've pitched and no matter how many years of service time are listed in your biography in the team media guide. Permission to succeed . . . Despite my status as an All-Star early in that '93 season, Torre still offered some lessons worth learning.

As I digest this even today, there is a second perspective, too, and that is of a young guy who battled his entire career to earn a permanent place in a major league rotation and then became really good . . . and then had to deal with that success. No matter the age or experience level, to grow from a struggling kid who grew up in a mobile home and now was an All-Star earning $2 million a year . . . to me, this was beyond my wildest dreams. My first incentive clause was playing for a win in Little League so the coach would take us to McDonald's. Suddenly, life and dollars become so much larger than a cheeseburger. And there are so many players today who came from those kinds of humble beginnings to earn far greater salaries. It plays in your head. *Am I really this good? I can't believe I'm making this much money, and if I do really well, I could make a lot more.* Talk about a disconnect between my self-image carved from my childhood and struggle to reach the majors and my current place in the game . . .

At some point, people perform on the field and in the workplace to their level of self-image. You see it in golf all the time. No matter the handicap of the golfer, a really good front nine score almost always is followed by a really poor back nine, which falls right into the player's handicap number. And vice versa. That's why Orel Hershiser's record streak of throwing fifty-nine consecutive innings in 1988 is so amazing. At some point, he didn't think, *Okay, well, nineteen innings is good, but what if... or, Okay, cool, thirty innings is good, but a few more...* No, he clearly maintained his focus on the matter at hand, the next pitch, the next hitter, the next inning, until that number became so ginormous that, nearly thirty years later, we still view it as a classic work of art, like a Chagall or a Rembrandt. Self-concept, the personal water level that keeps so many of us in check, is developed over many years with multiple influences. Socioeconomic, environmental and parental are chief among them. We develop certain positive and negative beliefs about ourselves, and these are the basis for our consistency. So when you hear that a person's reach should be greater than his grasp... well, sometimes that needs to be taught. Or learned.

That's part of what came out of Torre's office on that May day in 1993, as well. To my idea of "permission to be successful," Torre employs a word that he leaned on heavily with Derek Jeter, Mariano Rivera and assorted other key members of his Yankees dynasty teams. Trust.

"It comes down to the trust part of it," he says. "If you trust that a guy knows what he's doing, then you basically know that if the situation becomes a little stressful, that the game is not going to speed up for him. And that was Tewksie. He could handle pitching in key situations because he kept the game at a manageable pace for himself. There's a certain trust involved. I like to say that you may take somebody out and bring a fresh arm in, but that guy who you're going to take out, if that trust and belief in him exists, sometimes 80 percent or 70 percent of that guy is better than somebody else.

"I know it's important to use statistics, but that's why, for a manager, it's much more important in my mind to know your players. Sometimes those stats are accumulated and they don't really tell the whole story."

Sometimes, a fastball meant to be down doesn't land where you want it. Sometimes, your wife and kids are late to their seats because they are delayed by the president of the United States' motorcade. Small and large, thoughts become things. Always, it takes work to eliminate all those things that become distractions to knocking off the next task you've got to accomplish on the field, at the job or in the classroom. When Torre was hired as the Cardinals' manager in 1990, he came from the broadcast booth and it had been nearly six years since he managed a game, in 1984, for the Atlanta Braves.

"It was an important time for me because I had been away from managing for so long and, basically, he won my first game in St. Louis," Torre remembers.

That was on Thursday, August 2, in Philadelphia against Nick Leyva's Phillies. Torre took over in the series finale from interim manager Red Schoendienst, and I worked five innings and held the Phillies to two runs in a 4-3 win.

Over our next four seasons together, with Torre in the manager's seat, I won sixty-one games and grew exponentially in both the physical and the mental games. And I wasted as little time as possible doing it.

"He would be a joy right now for me in my position because we're concerned about game times and he didn't mess around," Torre, now chief baseball officer for Major League Baseball who oversees, among other things, pace of game issues, says with a chuckle: "He got the ball and he threw the ball. He had a game plan. He had his good control.

"You knew he was a journeyman-type pitcher, but he was so much more than that for me. The one thing I always felt that's unique in our game is that you get to know your individuals. And when you get to know your individuals, you have a better sense of what's going to benefit them and how you can help. Tewksie was easy, he had that fire in his belly and that's the one thing you need to have in this game because if you don't care a great deal, it's going to show up. It's going to expose itself."

From his office in the game today, Torre sees a good fit as I've graduated to my second career, applying what I've learned and studied over these years as a mental skills coach.

"First of all, Tewksie is a very caring individual," Torre says. "He's cerebral, he's an artist type, he does sketching and stuff. He wants to know why. He's got some thoughts on how to prepare, and all that stuff. So really, it didn't surprise me. In fact I was happy to see him in that capacity because when you leave this game, it leaves such a void. Especially if you did well and now, all of a sudden you're going to go work in a job completely separate. It's not that easy. The lifestyle in our game is unlike pretty much anything you do for a living. It's a sport, but it's more a game of life because you play it so often and so long. It doesn't possess the highs and lows of football, basketball, hockey, where you play two or three times a week, or once a week. You play 'em every day."

Which leaves a whole lot of things to figure out.

8

From Bird Seed
to Mind Food

When I walk into a minor league clubhouse, the scenes repeat themselves time after time. Baseball travel bags scattered across the floor of the musty locker room. Carpet dirtied with chunks of clay, the residue of dozens of spikes clomping across the floor. Crumpled paper cups littering the area near the wastebasket, so many missed "basketball shots." Potato chips, pretzels, peanut butter and jelly laid out on a table. Players anywhere from the ages of eighteen to twenty-seven with hope in their eyes and hunger in their hearts.

Today, I am in the visitors' clubhouse at Northeast Delta Dental Stadium in Manchester, New Hampshire, and you can smell the peanut butter. I'm visiting the Portland Sea Dogs, the AA affiliate of the Boston Red Sox, and they are here in Manchester to play the Toronto Blue Jays' Double-A team, the New Hampshire Fisher Cats. It is midseason, a time when the grind of the minor league schedule starts to have its effect on the psyche of the players. So before the team goes out for pregame batting practice, I ask them to sit for a minute. I am curious to see what state of mind the players are in.

"Hey, how many of you guys feel like you are playing up to your potential?" I ask.

No player raises a hand.

So I go on to explain to them the three key pillars of performance. One is physical—weight training, cardio work, the obvious. One is fundamental—hitting, throwing, fielding, the things you practice on the field. And one is mental.

Then I ask for a show of hands. "How many of you think the reason you are not playing up to your potential is because of something physical?"

No hands go up.

"Okay, is it something fundamental that is keeping you from playing up to your potential?"

A couple of players slowly, tentatively raise their hands.

"How about this," I ask. "How many of you think that the reason you're not playing up to your potential is because of something mental?"

They all raise their hands.

This is the maddeningly elusive part of the game. Suddenly, the blueprint becomes fuzzy. The directions become murky. In just about every other area, you can quantify your work. In a slump at the plate? Come in early tomorrow and take a hundred swings in the cage as the hitting coach keeps close watch and spoon-feeds tips. Fielding not as sharp as you would like? The infield coach is available to hit a hundred ground balls to you in a private tutoring session before batting practice this afternoon. Running out of fuel as fatigue sets in toward the end of a long season? Add more pounds as you lift weights this winter and increase your cardio work to make yourself stronger.

But what if, amid the scattered potato chips and strewn Gatorade cups and surrounded by more talent than you've ever before competed with, you suddenly begin to have this inexplicable, gnawing feeling that your dream is slipping from your grasp? And, worse, what if you don't know what to do about it?

For nearly every single player, by the way, that's not "if" but "when." At some point, everybody's career encounters turbulence.

This is a really hard game. From the year the National League was founded in 1876, only slightly more than 19,000 players have dressed for even one major league game. Statistics show that of roughly 483,000 boys currently playing high school baseball, only 1 in 47 will play Division I baseball, and only 1 in 764 will play major league baseball.

In almost every case, whatever level of professional ball, from Class A to The Show, growing up, each individual player has been the very best on his team. And he's become accustomed to that. Yet, sign a pro contract on the dotted line, report to rookie ball in Elizabethton, Tennessee, or Billings, Montana, or some other outpost where it seems as if you're living on the edge of the world and suddenly, the room is filled with guys every bit as talented as you. Every bit as decorated as you. And, in almost every case, just as insecure.

Always in these incredibly competitive environments, everybody is worried about something. Write that down in permanent ink. Sometimes it's obvious, sometimes not. I've always felt that players' obsessions with taking extra batting practice and watching endless video has as much to do with calming their own anxieties as anything mechanical in their swings.

And there is so much more. Maybe the mind is churning because a guy is feeling soreness in his arm for the very first time. Maybe it's because the player he's competing against for the second-base job suddenly has gone on a hitting tear over the past ten days. Maybe geography is putting a strain on the relationship a guy has with his high school girlfriend now that they're separated for the first time. Maybe it's making the next car payment that's due.

You don't simply flip open a computer and watch video to get a handle on these things.

I tell players that nobody goes into your room with a syringe, sticks you with a needle and withdraws your talent and your confidence. You do not lose your talent (at least, not until you're in your late thirties). What you sometimes lose is the perspective of what's going on *around* you and *to* you. Confidence always is on a continuum; that is, it's always moving up or down. Certainly, there are times during a season when you *feel* more confident than at other times. And, usually, in a results-based game, those times are based on—all together now—*results*. But . . . true confidence isn't based on results. No. Real, authentic self-confidence is the realization that you ARE a good player and that you believe in and trust yourself and your ability, even when the results are not what you desire. Often, individual expectations at the elite level are unrealistic. Nobody gets a hit *every* time, or makes the perfect pitch *every* time. A player is not awful when he strikes out or throws a meatball. True confidence is the realization that when things are challenging, you know that you have the internal resources not only to cope with those times but to overcome them with time, effort and persistence.

Confidence is a feeling, but it comes and goes. It is drained when players fail to meet their often unrealistic expectations. It is improved by thinking good thoughts and remembering past successes. A negative thought never leads to a positive result.

"I was giving him some trash about how long he pitched with the stuff he has, but you've definitely got to be super smart to survive in this jungle with it," says retired slugger David Ortiz, whom I first met as a teammate with the Minnesota Twins when he was twenty-two and I was thirty-seven, before we both moved to the Boston organization. "I always thought that he was special."

In the winter of 1998–1999, after thirteen seasons in the majors and at thirty-eight years old, I decided I'd had enough. The seeds of that decision were firmly planted toward the end of the '98 season when Laura and the kids went home to New Hampshire to start another school year and I was left alone in Minnesota. It had been a tough year in that I was on the disabled list for five weeks at midseason, we finished 70-92 and I went 0-4 with an 8.46 ERA in September.

After talks with the Boston Red Sox and Philadelphia Phillies fell through that winter—eliminating the idea of playing closer to home—in order to finish the physical education degree I had started eighteen years earlier at Saint Leo College, I applied to New England College in Henniker, New Hampshire. (The only Henniker in the United States! And, the game of paintball originated there in 1981! Go win a bar bet with those nuggets, on me.) Enough time had elapsed that suddenly it was Saint Leo University. A promotion?

Over lunch in Boston one afternoon that winter with Laura and me, Dan Duquette, the Red Sox general manager at the time, offered me a job as pitching coach at Class A Lowell. While appreciative of the offer, I was not interested. I had retired to spend more time with my family, and if I wanted to chain myself to the grind of another baseball schedule the next summer, I would have pitched for another season. At least the pay would have been far better.

One thing I did mention to Duquette, though, was this. I told him that in my observations, I thought there was a need for players to have some sort of mentor, especially in the minor leagues. And I told him I'd like to be involved with that, though I didn't want to jump right into the deep end immediately so soon after my retirement. So, he hired me as a pitching consultant who would work with Boston's top prospects at the Double-A and Triple-A levels. I did this from 1999 to 2003, and one spring as things slowly were beginning to change culturally in the game, I met a man named Doug Gardner who was working with the Red Sox minor league players as a sports psychology consultant (Doug had completed his doctorate in education from Boston University). He sparked my interest in that field and told me about his path toward a degree in developmental studies and counseling at Boston University.

Hmmm . . . I had devoured the *Greatest Salesman in the World* years ago, and I had even sold the author a pair of shoes. There were the audio self-help books featuring lessons on breathing and daily affirmations that I believed changed me from the inside out. There were thirteen postgraduate seasons in the majors featuring some of the diamond's greatest instructors, men like Catfish Hunter, Ted Simmons, Joe Torre, Bruce Bochy and, yes, Lou Piniella. There was my own active (and, yes, sometimes overactive) mind.

I started thinking about obtaining my master's degree in sports psychology and counseling from Boston University. It seemed like a great idea, except for two things: It wasn't something you earned overnight; this would take a bit. And I wasn't exactly enamored with the thought of spending several thousands of dollars on my degree knowing I had my children's college tuition and expenses coming up on the horizon.

And then, I visited our Triple-A affiliate in Pawtucket.

What started out as a very normal drive to a destination just two hours south of my home ended up with a mad overnight dash to New York City. One of the players confided in me that he was using cocaine, and he wanted help. It caught me totally unprepared. My immediate reaction was to tell him to contact the Red Sox employee assistance program, but the player didn't want to speak with the person in charge. So I called Dr. Joel Solomon, the medical director of the MLB Players Association, for guidance. I knew Joel well through many years of our involvement in the MLB Rookie Development Program that is held every January.

Now, here is the key element to this. I spoke to Joel, and not to the Red Sox, because in the role I was in (and would be for years to come), it was essential that I earn and keep the trust of the players. Without that bond, the position I was in would be as effective as lipstick on a pig.

So Dr. Solomon asked whether I could get the player to New York for an appointment the next morning at eight. I told him absolutely, and once that evening's game ended the player and I drove through the night to get to New York. We checked into the hotel around three in the morning, got up at seven-thirty and made it to the office for the eight o'clock appointment . . . and then I drove the player all the way back to Pawtucket in time for batting practice that afternoon.

I still vividly recall driving back to Rhode Island with the player sleeping in the seat next to me and my mind whirring. Should I have told the team? What would my relationship be with the players if I did? What kind of follow-up appointment is this player going to have with the doctor? As thoughts fired like pistons, one thing was as clear as the miles of asphalt in front of me. Despite my eighteen years of professional experience in baseball, the ups, the downs, the surgeries, the strategies, the hopes, the fears and the successes and struggles, while I certainly was qualified to help with any number of on-the-field situations, maybe the sum of my experiences still left me unprepared for helping a player with off-the-field challenges.

Yep, it was time to pull the trigger on applying to Boston University to both enhance and supplement my real-world education.

So, I applied in 2003, hit overdrive and graduated with honors in 2004, earning a master's degree in sports psychology and counseling.

In 2005, I started work as a mental skills coach in the Red Sox's minor league system while also working as a pre- and postgame television analyst for the New England Sports Network, something I had started in 2003 and enjoyed very much. It was a perfect avenue through which to bridge my playing career with whatever I would do next, and in a way it was not unlike pitching. I had to prepare ... same as for facing opposing hitters. I had to be on ... same as when I was on the mound. I was on the air during the 2004 miracle comeback against the New York Yankees in the American League Championship ("Soon it will be over," *Boston Globe* columnist Bob Ryan wrote when the Yankees raced out to that 3 games to 0 lead, "and we will spend another dreary winter lamenting this and lamenting that") and I saw the Sox break the eighty-six-year-old Curse of the Bambino from the broadcast perspective. What a time to have joined the Red Sox organization.

With the master's degree, though, it also was time to make a choice. And much as I loved the television work, working to understand the human mind had been a lifelong mission and passion for me—whether, at times, I knew it or not. At this point in my life, I knew it.

"Tewks has a lot to be proud of," says Brian Sabean, San Francisco's executive vice president of baseball operations and, like me, a native of Concord, New Hampshire. "He's blazed a trail, being an ex-player and going out later in life agewise to go back to school and take a completely different path.

"Baseball, to me, was the last sport to really embrace the mental skills side, and Boston was one of the first to do it. He was one of the first. He's a great guy. He could do anything in our sport he wanted to."

Among my key duties early on was taking a deep dive into the lower levels of the minor leagues in Boston to get to know the youngsters who had just been drafted or signed. Lester, Rizzo, Jonathan Papelbon, Dustin Pedroia, Kevin Youkilis, Clay Buchholz, Jacoby Ellsbury, Jed Lowrie, Josh Reddick and Ryan Kalish are among those who came through the Red Sox system as I was doing this work. Holy Johnny Pesky, what a crew.

With each conversation, the importance of trust was magnified even further. This is where relationships begin, and there are no shortcuts. Build a house or build a relationship, you cannot fake a strong foundation.

"You hear about some guys in some organizations that are pipelines, straight to the front office with what this guy's thinking, what he's doing," Anthony Rizzo says. "Tewks played, he's won a hundred-plus games, he's lost a hundred-plus games. That's a great career. He's been an All-Star, he's been sent up and down [seven] times, right? He has credentials. He's very easy to talk to and he understands that this is not easy. He understands that when you suck, it sucks for you and sometimes it sucks for everyone around you. He really helps control and helps you talk about all that stuff."

Rizzo was seventeen years old when the Red Sox drafted him in the sixth round in 2007 out of Stoneman Douglas High School in Parkland, Florida. Lester was eighteen when he joined the Boston organization as a second-round pick in 2002 out of Bellarmine Preparatory School in Tacoma, Washington. I met both of them shortly after they joined the organization.

Sometimes, a player and I will make a connection fairly quickly. Other times, as with Lester when he approached me six years into his big-league career, at twenty-nine, maybe the early seeds planted in a relationship bloom later. We all take different paths, and there is no one route to success.

Among baseball's universal truths, though, are these. For a starting pitcher, the moment his feet hit the floor to piss in the morning upon waking up on the day of his start, it can be extremely difficult to keep the mind from wandering and visiting negative spaces. For position players, if they have fallen into a slump or don't play for a few days, same thing.

The history of the game is littered with players who burst onto the scene as shining stars and then fade away, only to begin the rest of their lives' journeys in search of who they once were because they are so uncomfortable with who they are in the present. Many players don't even know how to handle failure because they were stars at every level from T-ball through high school or college before running into a wall at some point in their professional lives. Because, well, they are facing the best competition in the world. As former manager Jim Leyland likes to say of a big-league pitcher who has had a bad day: "Hey, the hitters drive Cadillacs, too."

Harvey Dorfman, one of the early pioneers in sports psychology and whose work with the 1989 Oakland Athletics and 1997 Florida Marlins earned him a couple of World Series rings, writes in *The Mental Game of Baseball* that "the greatest obstacle on the road to confidence is fear." There is fear of embarrassment, losing, disappointing your family . . . we could go on for the rest of the week. In a nutshell, though, it all boils down to this: Fear of failing.

FEAR is the acronym for "false evidence appearing real." The fear comes from the uncertainty of performance before you take the field. Pitchers don't know whether or not they will pitch well, for example. Or if they will win or lose. There is uncertainty of the outcome, and that uncertainty for a pitcher lacking confidence creates fear. When fear creeps in, self-talk becomes focused on what will go wrong if the pitcher doesn't pitch well. *My statistics will look like someone ran them through a shredder. My spot in the rotation may disappear.* Pitchers thinking like this allow their minds to control them rather than the other way around. The mind creates all of these destructive consequences that may happen to the pitcher if he doesn't pitch well. *I'll never make it to the major leagues. I'm going to get cut from the team. My college scholarship is in jeopardy. Dad is going to scream at me.* Instead of thinking of his next pitch, and then his next hitter, and then his next inning, the pitcher has caved to all of this garbage. Look, confident athletes battle fear, too. But they control it rather than allow it to control them.

The key to this is self-awareness. Players need to pay enough attention to this so they can identify what makes them uncomfortable during a game and work hard to change it.

Is a pitcher's confidence dented by a bad warm-up? By a walk? An error? A poor call by an umpire? Pitching with runners in scoring position? Maybe he doesn't like pitching in the cold. Or day games. Or night games. Whatever, when players lose confidence or feel uncomfortable, their inner dialogue changes, veering toward the negative and self-defeating. And that leads to the exact performance the player is attempting to avoid.

Whether I am sitting down with a minor league player next to the table containing the peanut butter and jelly sandwiches or whether I am standing with a major league player next to a spread that includes chicken parmigiana and grilled salmon, among the most important topics is self-talk. No, not what I'm doing with the player in that moment. Rather, what the player needs to be doing with himself out on the field, especially when the pressure builds and the game speeds up.

Inner dialogue should be focused on what the player wants to do in a situation and *not* on what he doesn't want to do or doesn't want to happen.

For example, early in the 2013 season, one of our minor league players in Boston was struggling badly at the plate. Today, José Iglesias is an All-Star shortstop with the Detroit Tigers. But as I talked with him nearly every day he was in Triple-A Pawtucket, early in the '13 season, and he was scuffling to keep his batting average above .200, I explained to him how we each have two voices, one over each shoulder, and we need to tune out the negative voice and focus on the positive voice. The Little Men, I call these voices. To those of you of a certain age, close your eyes and recall the scene from *National Lampoon's Animal House* in which Pinto is faced with, um, a decision, and a devil appears over his right shoulder urging him to do one thing and an angel appears over his left shoulder urging him to do another. Uh-huh.

"Earlier when I got there, I was making fun of him, I thought it was funny," Iglesias says. "But it makes sense. He always says you have two little men. One on your left shoulder and one on your right shoulder. One is a good guy and one is a bad guy. So it's which one you want to listen to. You have one guy telling you one thing and another guy telling you another thing, and it's which one you want to listen to, which one you want to be."

Already, Iglesias was frustrated at the time because, while he had broken camp with the big club, the Sox had demoted him two weeks into the season. Then, when he wasn't hitting in Pawtucket, he really became at risk to allow the demons to take over.

"We talked almost every day," Iglesias says. "He reminded me that I was a good player, just going through the process. He asked me a lot of things, we communicated really well and he sent me some videos, some positive videos."

Everything was designed not only to reinforce to José that he was a good player, but to remind him of it at certain checkpoints along the way, too. Though he teased me early, eventually I was able to get through to him that positive self-talk is no small thing. At the very least, it chases away the negative self-talk.

"Let's say you a hit line drive right to someone and you feel bad about it," Iglesias says. "And the little man is all, 'You see, this game sucks. This game is not fun.' And the other guy is like, 'It's fine, it's fine, you gotta get them next at-bat.' And you have to choose which one you want to listen to."

Once players begin to understand this part of the mental game, that choice is a slam dunk. Iglesias was twenty-three when we worked so hard together to get him through those early bumps in 2013. Now sailing toward his late twenties, he still carefully concentrates on these concepts in his game today.

"Absolutely," he says. "You're living that every day, day in and day out, in baseball so why not think about it and stay positive?"

In fact, talk about having fun with it. Iglesias not only thinks about it, he's drawn mental pictures of what the Little Men who comprise his inner voices look like. You bet the artist in me can appreciate *that*.

"I know that the bad guy is ugly," Iglesias says, eyes twinkling as he chuckles. "The other guy is pretty good looking, green eyes and everything. He speaks Spanish. The bad man talks to me in English, but the good guy speaks in Spanish so we get along.

"The good guy is on my right shoulder, on my throwing shoulder, and also speaks Spanish. He's bilingual. The bad guy speaks English and a little Spanish, not great, but Tewks Spanish. Just like him in Spanish."

Well, maybe I don't quite fully appreciate that last part!

Some self-talk involves anchor statements designed to help keep a player grounded when the storm fronts move through. Cleveland closer Andrew Miller, who had a breakout October during Cleveland's run to the 2016 World Series, came to Boston in 2011, when he was twenty-six and his head was still spinning from two trades that sent him from Detroit to Florida (in the Miguel Cabrera blockbuster) and then from Florida to Boston (a one-for-one deal for a left-hander named Dustin Richardson). We worked together to put a program in place that included an audio tool and some anchor statements that Miller still uses today.

Those anchor statements are a tool to help direct a player's focus to something positive when he is fighting negative thoughts. When those attack, a player must have the means to change those thoughts so they don't become things. I still remember facing Alex Rodriguez in the Metrodome one night when I was with the Twins, and as I carefully walked the tightrope that was pitching to A-Rod, I told myself, *Don't hang this curveball.* Well, gee, guess what happened? Whack! By having a set of anchor statements in mind, a player can (1) be aware of the thought, (2) delete it, (3) take a breath and (4) insert an anchor statement to merge back onto the positive path. (The anchor statement "trust, confidence, conviction" helped Dodgers veteran Rich Hill regain control of his career.)

Much of this information already was in my head as I set out to begin this second career after I retired. Some of it wasn't. The baseball maze, the chemistry of the brain reacting to competition and the bat rack full of emotions and challenges that go with it—I had navigated so much of that already. But that overnight run to New York City with the player who was trying to kick the cocaine habit all those years before was so illuminating, leading me to recognize that I needed to be prepared on so many different levels because you simply never know what baseball, and life, will throw at you next.

"He's just a guy who understands everything about the game," Kalish, the "old" outfielder, says of our time together in the Boston organization. "Obviously, he had the mental skills tool, but he was very versatile. You could go to him with whatever your issue was. For me, talking about stuff outside the field was the stuff I'd talk to him about. I know other guys would use him for the mental approach to baseball. I was pretty solid I felt like, mentally. But dealing with my injuries throughout the years, and other stuff: Ladies, balancing lifestyles, that was the stuff that him and I would get into. And that's what was so cool because he was so rock solid on all those things."

This was when Kalish was just eighteen and new into the organization in '06.

"I had a high school girlfriend," he says. "We broke up. Obviously, there are cool high school sweetheart stories and whatnot, but at that time it was heartbreaking for me. He was the first guy who called. We just talked about, obviously, at that age I needed help reminding me that baseball is the outlet. That was the key focus. For me baseball ended up being my therapy. He was always the one shooting you the text saying, 'Hey, just keep going to the yard, keep doing your work.' Which was never really an issue for me, and it might not have been without him. But still, to have a guy who was the foundation for me.

"We met before anything, when I was drafted. Then a few years in, this stuff comes up and we already had a foundation. And he was such a big help during that time. That was, again, the versatility with Bob."

"When you're eighteen," Kalish says, "would you open up as much to someone you know hasn't played, or to someone you know has? For me, someone who has is a no-brainer. Now I'm ten years older so meeting people now and knowing they might have went to school only and maybe played baseball in high school is okay, but at that age he was just so right for everyone."

Just as different types of music or various works of art touch each person differently, there is no one size fits all in working to try to lead a heartbroken player like Kalish toward sunny skies, a sinking prospect like Iglesias toward positive voices or a seasoned veteran like Lester toward visualization. With time and practice, I've learned it is essential to incorporate several tools from one box, including positive video reinforcement, audio affirmations, imagery and self-talk. I incorporate some of the same skills that Olympic athletes and professional golfers and tennis players use, all designed to improve both confidence and performance in stressful situations.

Of those tools, none carry more weight than the combination of pitching for thirteen years in the majors plus earning a master's degree in sports psychology and counseling.

"That's what's unique about him," Sabean says. "It really, to me, ties the knot. He's got more instant credibility and more to offer if a player or staff is so inclined to engage with him because of his long career in baseball. As we know, pitching is the loneliest thing you can do."

9

Mound Games
and Mind Games

During the winter of 1984–1985, the then-California Angels contacted a professor at nearby California State University, Fullerton, named Ken Ravizza. In addition to his class load teaching applied sports psychology, Dr. Ravizza worked with the school's baseball team on sharpening its mental skills, particularly the pitchers. Fullerton, the Little School That Could, won the 1984 College World Series.

The Angels' pitching coach at the time, Marcel Lachemann, was friends with Fullerton coach Augie Garrido, and during the course of their conversations, Ravizza's work came up and Lachemann's interest was piqued. So Lachemann invited Ravizza to spring training in '85, and the Fullerton professor arrived with the mixture of eagerness and nerves that can quickly cross-pollinate when you're invited into a brand-new territory but remain wholly unsure of the landscape.

It didn't take him long to find out that the cactus needles in the spring training desert could be awfully prickly.

"Gene Mauch was the manager of the Angels at the time, and it was really fascinating," Ravizza says. "Because the first time I went to spring training and Marcel introduced me, Gene said to me crystal clear: 'You are not here because I want you here, you are here because Marcel wants you here. And you stay away from my position players and just work with the pitchers.'"

Not exactly "Welcome, make yourself at home, and we left some chocolate mints on your pillow." But that was the culture in baseball at the time, and this was the atmosphere we needed to change. Why wouldn't a manager or a club want to use every single resource it could tap into? As with smartphones and GPS, the mental skills component of baseball for many players today is leading into a new age of enlightenment that begs the question, How did we ever live before these things were available to us?

"Back in the day, that was the culture in general," Jon Lester says. "As far as men were concerned, you weren't supposed to show any emotion other than that you were tough. Anything that allowed a supposed weakness in was viewed as making you weak. It's taken a long time for this game to evolve into 'Hey, you need to get your rest, you need to eat right, you need to do this, you need to do that to perform.' I think that's why now that we're out of the steroid era, you're seeing guys taking care of their bodies a lot more. I still feel there's a little bit of that stigma. I think every year it goes away a little more, but I still feel it's there for some guys. I think some guys look at others like, 'You're a whack job because you need to go talk to this guy.'

"I think it will dwindle down. You see more teams getting guys like Tewks involved with the big-league team and minor league program. It'll take time just like anything else. Like when guys started eating better, there were some who said, 'This guy's a wuss because he's not eating steak and potatoes, he's not staying up until 3 A.M. drinking.' It's like anything else, it takes time. The more teams that get involved with it, the more guys are going to buy into it and then it will get to the point where, 'Okay, it's just like another scouting report that you're doing.' That's what it's like for me now, just part of my routine, another fallback as far as being prepared for the start."

The godfather of modern mental skills work in baseball is the late Harvey Dorfman, who died in 2011 at the age of seventy-five. Though he earned a master's degree in educational psychology from the College at Brockport, part of the State University of New York system, he was not a psychologist. Rather, he taught college courses and authored several stories as a freelance writer, including some in which he interviewed baseball players on the game's mental side. His work led him to meet a man named Karl Kuehl, a baseball lifer who worked in player development and coaching for the Montreal Expos, Minnesota Twins, Philadelphia Phillies and Oakland Athletics. In the 1980s, as strength and conditioning programs were just moving into the forefront of the game, Kuehl was on the cutting edge of sharpening the brain while so many were focused on toning the muscles. In 1984, he hired Dorfman to work with the Athletics.

"He was in uniform, he was on the field with the guys, he was really great at relationships with coaches and players," Ravizza says. "He always had a story. Harvey was great for stories. One of his things was, if you don't have a story, make one up. He had a great sense of humor. The guys really liked him. He really fit in with the baseball community."

Dorfman and Kuehl coauthored the seminal book on the subject, *The Mental Game of Baseball: A Guide to Peak Performance* in 1989, and Dorfman became a Pied Piper of sorts to various players over the years, including Roy Halladay, Bob Welch, Al Leiter, Rick Ankiel, Brad Lidge and many, many others. His work earned him World Series rings from the Athletics in 1989 and from the Florida Marlins in 1997. He also worked with the Tampa Bay Devil Rays.

I can't remember when I met Harvey for the first time, but I certainly *knew* of him well in advance of that first meeting. In his book *Each Branch, Each Needle*, published in 2010, Dorfman writes that it was my friend and former teammate, catcher Terry Steinbach, who introduced us. "An All-Star who was plagued by a shoulder that caused his performance to be less than what it might otherwise have been, he compensated for the physical deficit by enhancing his mental approach," Dorfman writes. He also adds: "After he had graduated, I received a letter from his advisor and teacher at B.U., thanking me for sending such a fine fellow and thanking me for my mentoring. (Tewks undoubtedly exaggerated)."

Absolutely no exaggerations were necessary where this man was concerned. I read the *Mental Game of Baseball* and *The Mental ABC's of Pitching* while I was playing, both of which I still peruse from time to time just to freshen up on mental skills as I work with players. As I was finishing my master's degree and moved into my new career, Harvey told me that my pitching career would be both "a blessing and a curse." The blessing was that it would open doors and I would have instant credibility. The curse? I would need to think as a mental skills coach and not as a former player when working with a player. Because of my pitching experiences, it would be easy for me to give advice or counsel as a former player. The challenge would be to *not* look at things that way, but from the view of a mental skills practitioner.

He knew. He had already traversed the rocky path. The skeptics were rampant, especially at the beginning. If you were a sports psychologist back in the day, "You probably wouldn't have even gotten into the clubhouse," says Rich Donnelly, who coached for seven different big-league clubs since 1980 and is now retired. "Harvey Dorfman was a great motivational speaker, but when he came into the game the first time, we thought, 'Who is this freak?' Think of all the stuff we missed."

Think of all the stuff so many players missed over the past century or so of major league baseball. Long before Dorfman, Coleman Griffith, commonly remembered today as America's first sports psychologist, was hired by owner Philip K. Wrigley to work with the Chicago Cubs in 1938. That didn't go so well, however, when, according to the American Psychological Association's online magazine, manager Charlie Grimm openly mocked the "headshrinkers" and ordered his players not to cooperate with Griffith. Later that season, the Cubs fired Grimm and replaced him with catcher Gabby Hartnett. Griffith's early hopes that things would be different under a new manager quickly were dashed when the '38 Cubs were swept in the World Series by the New York Yankees. Hartnett, who would last only two more seasons as manager, didn't cooperate with Griffith, either. By 1940, Griffith was finished with the Cubs, nearly everyone in the game viewed his relationship with the team as a failure, and it wasn't until Dorfman and the 1980s that the game dared to ever so tentatively reexamine its approach to the mental game.

His advice to me was invaluable as an umpire with a generous strike zone in the late innings with runners in scoring position. I leaned on Harvey for control a lot early in my career as a mental skills coach. I would call him to talk about an issue with a player and how best to counsel that player. I also leaned on him personally. Many athletes struggle with the transition from playing to not playing. Even though I had retired on my own volition, there were periods of time in the first few years that were difficult for me. I would give Harvey a call, and it consistently helped. Always, he signed off the call by saying, "Be good to yourself." Those are words we all can, and should, remember. I miss his gruff voice filled with compassion and empathy but that, when needed, was also filled with directness and sternness. That's what made him so great, and we in the baseball world continue to miss him dearly today.

Though I worked with the Red Sox as their mental skills coach from 2005 to 2016 (minus the 2014 season, when I was with the Major League Baseball Players Association) before moving on to San Francisco, it wasn't until 2015 that Boston formally created a department of behavioral health. That same '15 season, under the guidance of former Red Sox general manager Theo Epstein, the Chicago Cubs established their own mental skills program which, according to the club, is "designed to assist major and minor league players with the mental aspects of baseball." Ravizza, whose relationship with Cubs manager Joe Maddon dates back to the 1980s, is one of their consultants.

Now, when Ravizza visits a clubhouse or speaks with a player, it is so much different from what it was in the mid-1980s, when he walked into a room and baseball people looked at him as if an exotic bird had just swooped down from the sky.

"At that time, it was very much like that," he says. "When Marcel brought me in for spring training that one time when I met Gene Mauch and all that went on, Marcel said, 'I'm going to give you half an hour and you can present your program to the pitchers. After half an hour, I'm going to give them three-and-a-half-by-five index cards and tell them to write yes or no on the cards, yes come back, or no get him out of here.'

"I can still remember that talk. It rained that day in Mesa and I had to move my talk to the back side of the old clubhouse. Guys were sitting on fertilizer bags, lime bags. I've got thirty pitchers in there and I'm as nervous as can be giving that talk. Then, in the middle of the talk, the hot water heater from the shower room goes on and this loud roar comes on in the room. To tell you the truth, I didn't even hear the roar, I was so focused. Finally I finished, and three or four guys came up to me and said, 'You didn't even hear the hot water heater come on.' I said, 'No, I didn't.' And they said, 'I can learn something from you.' That's baseball. Subtle things."

When Lachemann collected the index cards, only two were marked no. Ravizza had sold the Angels pitchers with his focus and his message. By the end of that spring, even the gruff Mauch was intrigued, at least, as much as he could be.

"It took a while, but I would say by the end of spring training, I could talk to anyone," says Ravizza, who, over the years, has worked with several college teams as well as consulted with the US Olympic program for their men's and women's volleyball, field hockey, baseball and softball. "Mauch was checking me out. In baseball, there's a lot of people pulling on those players."

Three years later, in 1988, Chicago White Sox owner Jerry Reinsdorf recruited a Rutgers University professor of applied psychology to work with his White Sox. At the time, the position in baseball was still so vague that Dr. Charlie Maher wasn't even sure what to make of it. He figured they wanted a consultant. But the White Sox, with Larry Himes running the club as general manager, told him no, they wanted someone to develop a mental skills program from rookie ball all the way up to the major leagues. Because Reinsdorf also owned the NBA's Bulls, Maher became involved with them, as well.

All of this was easier said than done because, while the ideas were there, the buy-in from the players wasn't.

"It was like, 'There's nothing wrong with us,'" Maher says. "The suspicion was, 'Oh, you're going to try to psychoanalyze us? Someone thinks we have a problem?' Many players thought that way. *I don't have a problem.* Coaches were even, 'I've been doing this for twenty years. I know what these players need. You're not going to tell me what they need.'"

The game still tilted hard toward the Wild West, more Clint Eastwood than Jake Gyllenhaal.

"Over the course of time, if you listened to them, once they trusted you they'd tell you what they need," Maher says. "We'd used more of what I would call an 'educational approach,' looking at the mental side, what things could go wrong and derail performance, what things could enhance performance."

Maher in those early days would conduct group meetings with players to discuss motivation and focus, what factors boosted those things and which factors limited them. What were the players' experiences like in those areas? The group discussions were designed to make it so the players did not feel like they were sitting on a psychiatrist's couch.

"That was the initial hump you had to get over," Maher says. "Some of that exists today, but it's very minimal. Players now are more open to and aware of what they need to do to get better. They recognize the importance of learning more about the mental side of the game and what they need to do."

In 1995, the Cleveland Indians spirited Maher away from Chicago and tasked him with creating an organization-wide mental skills program. Running the Indians at the time were GM John Hart and his assistants, Dan O'Dowd and Mark Shapiro. Coincidentally, Maher's first season with the Indians was also the first full season in the majors of one Manny Ramirez.

"One thing I could say is that, early on with the Indians, working with Manny Ramirez, I was very impressed with him," Maher says. "Here's someone who had, quote, 'limited formal education,' end quote, but he was somebody who was very disciplined. He wanted to learn about the mental side of the game. How to stay focused from pitch to pitch and learn more about himself. Maybe that's not the typical impression people have of him, but he was very oriented toward the mental side of the game. He took instruction and worked on it. He was really very intelligent, a guy who really worked on it."

Typically, Manny and Maher would meet one on one in a little office off the Indians' clubhouse, or on the dugout bench early before games. These meetings were not formal. "He was an individual who was not really oriented that way," Maher says. "But he was always asking questions, and he was honest with himself about how he was performing. He wanted to get his plan down to the very, very basics, to where he would see the ball and make solid contact, and be relaxed enough in the batter's box to be able to do that."

In his role with the Indians today, Maher is in charge of a department that includes the sports psychology program, the employee assistance program and the business psychology program. In a role that cuts across both baseball and business operations, he also does developmental work with members of the front office. Now a professor emeritus of applied psychology at Rutgers University, Maher nevertheless estimates that he spends 75 percent of his time in Cleveland. In fact, from 1999 to 2009, he also was the sports psychologist for the NBA's Cavaliers and NFL's Browns but gave those two jobs up because there simply wasn't time to cover three sports. Plus, it was too taxing on him.

"If someone would have told me back in the '90s that this was going to happen, I'd say this is crazy," says Maher, thinking back to the 1980s when he initially figured his role with the White Sox would be as a consultant and it would get him out of part of the New Jersey winter so he could spend time in spring training in Sarasota, Florida.

What that has evolved into is a postmodern program in Cleveland: an entire system designed by Maher that focuses on the mental and emotional development of players, coaches and staff members and concentrates on their development not only as players, but as people. This full-immersion program covers mental skills on the field, life skills off the field and also includes programs for substance abuse, education, nutritional counseling, financial management, even things as basic as managing an apartment (that part is designed more for lower-level minor-leaguers coming into rookie ball, or low Class A, and Latin players relocating into the United States). Plus, it covers mental health (assistance for players and their families), domestic violence, family counseling, occupational stress and, of course, preventative education on these topics. And this is all done in confidence.

Today, Maher is the president of our Professional Baseball Performance Psychology Group (PBPPG), which consists of persons who provide mental skills and related services in twenty-three of the thirty major league organizations. At least some of the seven other organizations employ some type of mental skills person who doesn't yet qualify for membership in PBPPG (criteria demands that members have earned a master's degree or higher in applied sports psychology plus a minimum of one year working in professional baseball).

Clearly, this is light-years beyond the grim tales of Charlie Grimm, or Mauch ordering Ravizza not to speak with any of his position players, only with the pitchers. Cutting-edge clubs today understand that developing the complete player is beneficial to all, not just focusing on his hand-eye coordination in drills or muscle mass in the weight room.

Indians manager Terry Francona, with whom I worked closely when we both were in Boston's organization, first saw the value of this kind of work from a man named Don Kalkstein when Francona was the bench coach for the Texas Rangers in 2002. Kalkstein that season was working with the Rangers players, and today he is the director of sports psychology for the NBA's Dallas Mavericks and a consultant for the Rangers.

"He kind of taught me the value of having someone around," Francona says.

Francona is old school enough to know that anything having to do with mental skills would have been viewed as a weakness back when his father, Tito, played in the majors (1956–1970) and, largely, when he played (1981–1990). But from Texas to Boston to Cleveland, the old-school manager who connects so well with today's players understands the value.

"We work our fielding, our throwing and our hitting," Francona says. "But the mental side might be the most important tool. If you view it as a weakness, that's silly. It's like, you can do better. So we're trying. If you don't, you're kind of missing the boat. There are ways to get better."

In an industry that earns more than $10 billion in revenues annually, the competition is so fierce that even the slightest, most fractional edge can become incredibly valuable. It's why the whole "moneyball" thing blew up in the early 2000s. Billy Beane and the Oakland A's were able to identify a market inefficiency and take full advantage. Today, every club owns a high-powered magnifying glass and searches for the slightest crack in the market. As analytics and forward thinkers continue to push and prod the game into the postmodern era, the goal is to ensure that there is nothing we miss. Combine that with the fact that perhaps some of the people working with players today have evolved over time and are better equipped to understand needs specific to baseball players as opposed to, say, those of a downhill skier. And just as the science of nutrition has become an area in which teams know they can gain an edge on their opponents, so, too, is the science of sports psychology.

As most executives running baseball teams now believe, when seven o'clock arrives on a typical weekday during the season, the better a player feels—his *full* body and mind—the better chance he has to perform. And while players ultimately are responsible for this, teams had better understand they have a responsibility for providing resources to ensure that when the first pitch is thrown each night, players are feeling good fundamentally from the proper coaching, and that their minds are right, too.

For example, the Cubs employ a "director, mental skills program," a "Latin coordinator, mental skills program" and a "coordinator, mental skills program." Epstein notes that one key is that a club must have a manager who is all in, and the erudite Maddon, who always has been ahead of his time, certainly is. Just like Francona and a growing list of other managers.

"Teams are competing on the field," says Ben Cherington, the former Boston GM who was in place when the club created its department of behavioral health in 2015. "It's intense competition, so teams are trying to find any area for advantage in that competition. Obviously, A no. 1 is always going to be, How talented are the players on the field? That's going to drive your success more than anything. It always has, and it always will. But teams aren't stopping there. You can find smaller areas, even a fraction of a percentage point advantage in some area that might give you an advantage. Even if it's just one win a year, wins are valuable. I think teams are looking for any area of advantage they can get.

"To that extent, there's been a change in society as well. Years ago, there was more of a taboo on it. To the average Joe working in a factory, a psychologist would be a stigma. Baseball, as well, has evolved."

In the old days, a Pittsburgh Pirates pitcher named Steve Blass went 19-8 with a 2.49 ERA in 1972 and helped pitch the Bucs into that fall's National League Championship Series (NLCS) against the Cincinnati Reds. Blass won one of two starts in the NLCS before the Big Red Machine moved on to the World Series. The next year, he completely and inexplicably lost his ability to throw strikes, and by 1975 he was out of baseball completely, and this particular version of the baseball yips that attacked him was even referred to as "Steve Blass disease."

An obvious mental tic like that is extreme, of course. But, yes, thankfully, baseball has evolved past the days when a player like Blass was left to his own devices and had a "disease" named after him. He isn't the only one over the years. Most notably and recently, Rick Ankiel, the former St. Louis pitcher, lost his promising career on the mound because of the same thing. Second basemen Steve Sax and Chuck Knoblauch suddenly lost their ability to throw to first base on ground balls, and Knoblauch quickly became the butt of jokes nationally when one of his throws sailed high up into the Yankee Stadium stands and hit the mother of political pundit Keith Olbermann.

Lester, as most baseball fans know, has difficulty throwing accurately to first base, which can leave him susceptible to opponents running games and bunts. I can still vividly recall Larry Lucchino, who was Red Sox president at the time, approaching me on the team charter flight to St. Louis to start the 2013 World Series, encouraging me to address Jon's throwing issues prior to his start.

"I talked to Tewks a little bit about it, but it really didn't become a big thing until I came over to the Cubs," Lester says.

Bottom line: Whether the issue is playing out like Ankiel in front of packed stadiums or whether it's something far more subtle, as we've advanced and become far better educated across all fronts in society and in sports, it screams "Irresponsibility!" if modern baseball does not try to help players with every tool at our disposal, including—and especially—in the mental skills area. There simply are too many resources available today.

"It's a very hard thing to train," Cherington says. "The training is not visible. If the shortstop needs to work on his back end, while there are very specific physical exercises he can do, a matter of reps, he can do it. I think the people that are working to help players with on-field mental skills, that group has evolved over time ... It's a little bit that the field has evolved, and a little bit that players hopefully recognize this is their progression, and if they want to excel at it and have a long career, they have an obligation to do whatever they can to put themselves in the best position to be successful. For some players, it might mean getting in better shape. For some, it might mean working on a particular skill. For others, it might mean working with some on-field psychology. Or, it could be all of those things."

The game has come a long way from when Dorfman was the Lone Ranger working with Oakland and a sort of Pied Piper as a mental skills coach, when individual players from various teams, like Roy Halladay, would seek him out on their own during the winter. And from the time when Doug Rader followed Mauch as Angels manager (1989–1991). You've heard of players getting optioned out to the minors? Rader sent Ravizza down.

"He said to me he didn't want me around the big-league team anymore," Ravizza says. "But what was great was, at the end of the year, Doug called me and said he had made a mistake, regretted it and wanted me to come back the following spring and work at all levels. It was great for me. I renegotiated my contract."

Plus, Ravizza learned a ton that summer, working with all of the minor-leaguers.

"When I look around today versus then, some teams have three or four mental skills people now, like the Cubs," Ravizza says. "They're really providing as part of the everyday process. Some of the teams are doing more with the psychological testing part of it to help with the draft. Some are moving in the direction of using a lot of technology, biofeedback equipment, brain waves stuff, some of that. At the same time, what's really key, what I've seen change, is that coaches and everyone are more receptive. You're able to integrate the mental game stuff into task-relevant performance keys. What do I mean by that? It's not just about relaxing, visualizing and imagery, it's how do you actually do one pitch at a time? One question I ask ballplayers is, 'When does the last pitch end and the next pitch begin?' Then you can start integrating when you need to think and when you need to react. Then you can start developing the player's system. It's not one system. A player has to develop his own system."

In our work today, I speak with Ravizza and Maher from time to time when issues or questions occur.

"What Bob brings to the table: Bob did it. He was there. He had his career," Ravizza says. "When Bob talks about the mental game, I listen, because, shit, man, he's walked the walk. I really have so much respect for him. When he was done with his career, he went to Boston University and got his degree from a really good program where he really had to know his stuff, and he did the work. There are times when I have questions, and I don't hesitate to call Bob and get his input."

Certainly, there is some experience that cannot be taught; it is earned. Particularly gratifying to me today is that from my field and clubhouse views during my playing days, an area in which I saw a clear need is under heavy construction now with both management and players becoming more enlightened than ever before.

"It's an area that's not going away," Maher says. "The organizations like the Indians are investing money in it because, hey, if we're dealing with the fundamental side of the game, the physical, how much are we investing? This is the next evolution, the solidification in the game of the mental side and services."

Ravizza chuckles at the old meetings he once conducted with Angels players at a Rodeway Inn motel in Mesa, Arizona.

"It's amazing when I see a lot of those ex-players, they always bring up the meetings we used to have there," he says. "I think if there's one thing in doing this work in baseball that's really gotten to me, it's the number of players you think may not be into it, but they're hearing what you say. Because sometimes in the clubhouse, in that culture, you can't let on that you're into it because you've gotta be macho, you've gotta be tough.

"But what's amazing is the number of guys I've seen either at games or in spring training and they tell me, 'Ken, I'm using that stuff now in my life even more than I did as a player.'

"Even some, I've talked to their children. They call now and say, 'Hey, Ken, would you be willing to talk to my son? Darin Erstad brings me in to talk to his team at the University of Nebraska."

10

Lefties in Their
Right Minds

The tall, bearded man stood in the shower, under a blast of hot water, alone with his thoughts. Before long, he would be asked to trot in from the bullpen, another postseason game on the line, another sell-out crowd roaring, another set of national television cameras shining the white-hot spotlight on him.

Soon, Andrew Miller, the breakout star of Cleveland's inspirational run to the 2016 World Series, would be doing his thing on the mound, firing devastating sliders at Mookie Betts or Edwin Encarnación, hurling his fastball at José Bautista or Kris Bryant, polishing off another strikeout of Russell Martin or Melvin Upton Jr. or Kyle Schwarber. By the end of that postseason, he would be selected as the Most Valuable Player of the American League Championship Series (ALCS). During the 2016 regular season, Miller struck out 45 percent of the 103 batters he faced while walking only 3.3 percent.

Each night, all of this started with Miller standing on a tile floor during his pregame ritual, steam rising all around, repeating to himself the first of his daily set of anchor statements. Then, at various times throughout the evening, from the shower to the dugout to the bullpen and, yes, to the mound, he made time to repeat those statements and toss in a few more. Through spring, summer and into fall, from before he was established through his October heroics and right up until now, his routine is the same, with minor tweaks here and there as the seasons go by.

"When we stand there for the national anthem, I'm kind of talking to myself," Miller says. "People might think I'm crazy or losing my mind or praying or something. But, in reality, I'm going through and telling myself those positive things that I want to think about before going into a game."

Miller was Detroit's first-round draft pick (third overall) in 2006, debuted for the Tigers that summer at twenty-one and was traded to Miami a year later in the monster, eight-player deal that sent slugger Miguel Cabrera to Motown. The Marlins traded him to Boston in 2010, the Red Sox shipped him to Baltimore at the July trade deadline in 2014 and, after that season, he signed a four-year, $36 million free-agent deal with the New York Yankees. The Indians acquired him at the July trade deadline in 2016 and, as injuries ravaged their rotation that autumn, Miller's versatility and dominance out of the bullpen were enormously important to manager Terry Francona in paving the way toward their first World Series appearance since 1997.

Like most relievers, Miller was a starting pitcher early in his career. But at six foot seven, his windup was a blur of moving parts and awkward angles that easily and often fell out of sync. The result was predictable. Too many walks on the field, and an erosion of confidence in his psyche. "I struggled in the major leagues, I was with a new organization and I had created a lot of bad habits," Miller says. "With that came a lot of negative thoughts and bad thought processes."

When we first met, Andrew was twenty-six, he had been acquired from the Marlins, where he had gone 1-5 with an 8.54 ERA in nine games (7 starts) and he still had designs on starting. The Marlins got a left-handed pitcher named Dustin Richardson in return. Notably, Richardson never played another game in the majors following the deal.

"When I came over to Boston I was in a place where I needed to refine that part of my game," he says. "It was something I wasn't doing very well. We kind of built something over time. It changed. I did some audio stuff he put together, we talked after starts for a while, we put together plans and worked on different things. What he and I did, we were all over the map, but it led to a pretty solid routine that I have now."

When we connected in "the Fort," Fort Myers, Florida, spring training home of the Red Sox, one of the first things he said to me was "I won one game last season. I mean, what pitcher does *that?*" Andrew had been knocked around on the field and bounced around enough off of it early in his career that he was battling the negative-thought demons an inordinate amount of the time. No doubt, he wasn't performing as well as he thought he *should* be or how others *expected* him to. It was obvious Andrew had been carrying around a lot of anger and frustration, and he was more than ready to do whatever he needed to improve his performance.

Over the course of that 2011 spring training, we made a plan to work on three aspects of his game. First, he needed to improve his self-talk, stopping with the negative thinking and rationalizing his poor outings with excuses to protect what was left of his confidence. Second, Andrew needed to improve his first-pitch strike efficiency. One constant in baseball for 135 years now is that working ahead in the count increases the pitcher's likelihood of getting the hitter out. And when that pitcher is six foot seven and throwing 95–97 m.p.h. from tough angles, hitting in a 1 and 0 count is far more comfortable than hitting when you're behind 0 and 1. Third, we needed to work on his focus to compete, especially early in the game. To have a greater sense of urgency, to get "checked in," as he called it, *before* he had some men on base and not *when* he had some men on base. Looking back, who knows, but perhaps working out of the bullpen was his destiny to begin with.

Andrew started that 2011 season in the Triple-A Pawtucket rotation, and his early success there—61 strikeouts in 65 innings pitched and a 2.45 ERA—warranted his recall to the bigs in June. However, upon reaching Boston, he again struggled with his command, walking 41 hitters in twelve starts. The final start of his big-league career came on September 8 in Toronto. Six days after he had started and surrendered six earned runs in 1.1 innings in a 10-5 loss to Texas, the Blue Jays ambushed Miller for five earned runs in 5 innings in a 7-4 Red Sox loss. Andrew's final three appearances that season were out of the bullpen and, as he struck out seven, walked three and surrendered three hits and two runs in 3.2 relief innings, that turned out to be a prelude to his pitching rebirth as an ace reliever.

For the Red Sox, that 2011 season came attached with one of the worst endings in major league history. After leading Tampa Bay by nine games in the wild-card chase on September 3, placing our odds of making the postseason at 99.6 percent, the month turned sour and the Sox were eliminated with a loss on a rainy September night in Baltimore's Camden Yards after the Rays had stormed to a come-from-behind win against the Yankees in Tampa. Not long after the season ended, so did the tenure of Tito Francona as Boston manager.

In the winter of 2011–2012, the Red Sox hired Bobby Valentine to replace him, many believing his personality was just what was needed to "fix" the clubhouse, a clubhouse the critics felt Francona let get away from him late in that 2011 season. Result? The Red Sox finished last in the AL East at 69-93, canning Bobby V after just one season.

But . . . out of the wreckage of '12, one of the bright spots to emerge was Miller's ascendance as a bona fide major league reliever. Andrew made fifty-three relief appearances that season, going 3-2 with a 3.35 ERA. Most importantly, his walks per nine innings decreased to a career low 4.5 and his strikeouts per nine innings leaped to 11.4.

The big lefty continued to soar the next summer, his strikeouts per nine catapulting up to 14.1. But, unfortunately, his newfound dominance was not available to us after he suffered a foot injury on a strange play in Anaheim in early July. "Lefty" tripped while running to back up home plate after a base hit, tearing some ligaments and putting him on ice for the rest of the season. I felt so bad for him. He was hitting his stride, pitching like he knew he could and then, *boom!* I can still picture this bearded giant maneuvering around the Sox's clubhouse on a scooter, his injured leg supported while he used the other leg to propel his large body where it needed to go. Nonetheless, he was there cheering for his teammates that entire postseason.

In 2014, Miller continued to improve his strikeouts per nine to 14.9 and lowered his walks per nine down to 2.5, but approaching free agency that winter, the Sox decided to trade him to Baltimore for Eddie Rodríguez, a promising young left-hander. By 2016, Miller was so good in so many spots for Francona and the Indians that he became the focal point of a national discussion regarding a potential revolution in the way in which relievers might be used in the game.

"I've worked with other people, but the stuff we put in place in Boston is what I'm still using today," Miller says. "It's a very important part of my success, or turnaround. It's something I take very seriously and I think it's had a big impact on my pitching."

The most important performance tool that helps keep Miller in a good place mentally is his use of positive self-talk in the form of what I call "anchor statements." These are short, positive statements used to replace a negative thought. I like to explain them to players by using a boat metaphor. If the player is on a boat in a lake without an anchor to keep the boat secure and a storm blows in, the boat will go wherever the winds take it. The mind is similar. If a player has no way to anchor the performance of his mind when a "storm" moves in, that performance likely also will blow in whichever way the wind takes it. And in a profession steeped in failure that naturally breeds self-doubt, it is important to delete a negative thought as quickly as possible and replace it with something positive.

Where do these negative thoughts come from? Psychologist Dr. Judith Beck calls them "automatic thoughts." I call that voice the Little Man, the negative, doubting, self-bashing inner voice that always is chirping at us, especially in moments when we don't feel particularly confident or comfortable. And this annoying voice is there in all of us. The golfer teeing off over a water hazard hears the voice. *Don't hit it in the water!* The tennis player faced with having to get a second serve over the net hears it. *Don't double fault!* This voice is not exclusive to athletes. During a business presentation. *I hope I don't screw this up. What will my boss think?!*

Vividly, I recall the Little Man getting me once before a game in San Francisco. I wasn't feeling particularly chipper as I was warming up prior to the game, and it didn't help that the bullpens in old Candlestick Park were on the field, adjacent to several rows of heckling Giants fans, who, over the course of my fifteen-minute warm-up, had pretty much zapped any confidence I had before I started warming up. Their voices funneled into my brain until the thoughts fired at me reflexively. As psychologist Beck says, these thoughts "are not the result of deliberation or reasoning. Rather these thoughts seem to spring up automatically; they are often quite rapid and brief. You may be barely aware of these thoughts; you are far more likely to be aware of the emotion that follows . . . as a result, you most likely uncritically accept your automatic thoughts as true." Often, they appear in shorthand, coded in just a few words or an image. No matter how off the wall, these thoughts almost always are believed, and the reason they are believed is because they appear as if programmed automatically. They always focus on the worst-case scenario, they're often couched in terms of *should, don't, can't, must.* And they also differ from public statements. For example, a player speaking with reporters after a game isn't going to say he served up a hittable, bases-loaded pitch because he was afraid to walk the hitter. He's going to say he fell behind in the count and had to come in with a pitch, and he just missed. Yeah, riiiiiight!

So I completed my warm-ups in Candlestick, walked down to the visitors' dugout, and as I was sitting there waiting to start the bottom of the first inning, the Little Man voice picked up in my head where those hecklers left off. *You're probably not even going to get out of the first inning tonight! You've got nothing! At least you can always become a physical education teacher!* I thought, *What? How crazy is this, my thoughts going from not pitching well to not pitching at all!*

The anchor statements Miller sprinkles into his days in order to keep storms like that at bay are a crucial part of who he is. When the howling winds blow in, his mind isn't being pitched all around the lake. It is why he is vigilant about his program, beginning in that pregame shower, repeating to himself, among other things: *I trust and believe in my stuff . . . I consistently see myself throwing strikes.* And, the one he finishes with: *I've done it before, I will do it again. I'll do it tonight. I'll do it right now.*

In the first two games of the ALCS against Toronto in '16, Miller fanned ten of the twelve batters he faced, including, at one point, five

167

in a row. He also became the first pitcher in MLB history to strike out five or more hitters on consecutive days, and over his first four appearances in the 2016 postseason, he struck out seventeen hitters in 7.2 innings pitched. In being named as the ALCS MVP, he worked 7.2 scoreless innings against Toronto, surrendering three hits and no walks while fanning fourteen. He set an ALCS strikeout record for relievers, earned one save, was credited with three holds and, to that point, had worked 20 scoreless innings to begin his playoff career. Throughout, he repeated the set of anchor statements that he and I put into place.

Though he has not developed any physical triggers to help him change a negative thought, Miller does recall something someone told him years ago, and that is to visualize a stop sign.

"The main thing is being aware of, 'Okay, I'm having these thoughts, it's not productive, it's not going to help me perform,'" he says. "How to control that, and turn them around.

"For me, and this was something big in talking with Tewks and others, we all have those thoughts from time to time. 'This isn't going to go well. I don't have it today.' I tell myself, 'Stop.' I try and change the thought to something positive, switch from 'I don't think I'll be able to do this today' to 'Stop. I've got this. I will dominate.'"

Early in my own career, I didn't know how to control this negative inner voice. It was as if my mind controlled me. As I trained myself over time, and it does take time, my ability to control the Little Man worked more often than not. During my All-Star season in St. Louis, I faced 915 batters over 233 innings pitched . . . and walked only 20 of them. The next summer, 1993, I faced 907 batters over 213.2 innings pitched . . . and again walked only 20.

According to the Elias Sports Bureau, the official statistics arm of MLB, among starting pitchers from 1920 on (minimum of 1,500 innings pitched), I rank second all-time in fewest walks per nine innings (1.42), trailing only Grover Cleveland Alexander (1.26).

Also, I started at least twenty games while averaging less than one walk per start six times in my career, including in my final season, 1998, when I made twenty-five starts and walked only twenty. Also according to Elias, the only other pitcher to accomplish that since 1900 is Hall of Famer Greg Maddux, who had fewer walks than games started in each of seven different seasons in which he started at least twenty games. Next on the list: David Wells (5), Bartolo Colón (5) and Brad Radke (5).

Now, none of this happened because I was never behind in the count. No, it happened because I worked hard on my mechanics, refining my ability to throw strikes at any time, in any count. And I came to understand that my mind, my thoughts, were often my biggest opponent. I worked hard to develop strategies to anchor my mind before my performance went where the winds took it.

Over time, I did develop a physical trigger to help exile the negative Little Man while bringing back the positive self-talk. Whenever the Little Man's voice appeared, I would take my glove hand and bang it against my left leg. It was my way to delete or erase the negative thought. I would walk off the back of the mound to the infield grass, take a deep breath in through my nose, filling up my lungs, hold it for a beat and then exhale slowly through my mouth. Then, I would reframe the negative voice into a more positive directive focused on the task at hand. *Okay, throw a good, low strike.* Or, *Just like in the bullpen.*

Says Miller: "I'm big on telling myself to stop thinking about bad thoughts when they come in, trying to shut it down as quickly as possible. Those are habits I think you can create. Eliminating the bad thoughts as quickly as you can is something that pays off, and telling yourself those positive things pays dividends as well.

"Baseball players tend to be creatures of habit. I don't want to say OCD [obsessive-compulsive disorder] because that suggests disorder. But I have quite a reliance on things as I go through my day, and that's part of it."

While self-talk is Miller's preferred tool, just like one of his '16 World Series opponents on the mound—Lester—he employs visualization as well.

"Absolutely," Miller says. "It fits into what all of us do, whether it's benefiting you or hurting you. Whether you think you are or not, you're absolutely visualizing, and I think visualizing positive things is certainly a better way to go out and perform."

The package continues to position Miller for success at an elite level, though the landscape continually changes, no two days are the same and the tall lefty must continue to keep a sharp eye out for potential disruptions to his concentration and anchor statements.

"At this point, one of the challenges to me is saying them with conviction, and not just going through the motions," Miller says.

Like so much else in life, his program remains a work in progress.

"I don't think anybody could ever claim to figure it all out," Miller says. "I'm sure there are people with doctorates in psychology who would say they haven't figured it all out. Now it's routine based for me, but I don't want to get too routine based to where it doesn't mean anything and I'm going through the motions. So my anchor statements have shifted from what they were a couple of years ago to what they are now."

I've done it before, I will do it again tonight . . .

One day before Miller did do it again—throwing two more shutout innings in Game 3 in another unconventional appearance designed by Francona to help finish Cleveland's sweep of Boston in the AL Division Series (working the fifth and sixth innings, striking out two)—Rich Hill started Game 2 of the NL Division Series for the Los Angeles Dodgers with three consecutive strikeouts, whiffing Trea Turner, Bryce Harper and Jayson Werth. Good morning, good afternoon and good night.

Though Hill would lose on that afternoon, nine days later he would outpitch Chicago Cubs ace Jake Arrieta to help the Dodgers take a 2 games to 1 lead in their National League Championship Series. Over six shutout innings, Hill was masterful, holding the Cubs to two hits and striking out six.

As the baseball world was glued to these riveting stories, I was riveted by the irony. When Miller and Hill were teammates at Triple-A Pawtucket in 2011, Hill was marooned in the bullpen and wanted to start, and Miller was in the rotation before the game led him to the bullpen.

The first time I met Rich was that season in a clubhouse in Buffalo, New York, where the PawSox were playing the Bisons, Triple-A affiliate of the New York Mets. The Chicago Cubs' fourth-round pick out of the University of Michigan in 2002, a series of injuries was part of the reason Hill wound up bouncing from the Cubs to Baltimore to St. Louis to Boston. All the while, he was trying to replicate his solid 2007 season in Chicago in which he went 11-8 with a 3.92 ERA in 195 innings pitched over thirty-two starts.

He had just joined the PawSox after starting out the season with the Cardinals' Triple-A team in Memphis. I didn't really know much about Rich other than he was from Milton, Massachusetts, so he had to be a good guy.

Hill thought I had an interesting background, and he thought since we both knew pitching there could be a connection. He was very open about his work with Harvey Dorfman—Hill had contacted him in 2005—and how much that had helped his mental game. Right then, I knew that he and I would click.

"He was great to talk to because he was straight to the point," Hill says of Dorfman. "That's how Tewks is, too, straight to the point. He tells you what he sees, and he calls you out on things. He makes you better as a player as you go along. The biggest thing I've found is that if a player continues to seek advice, seek help, there are people who can help that player get the most out of his potential on the baseball field."

We all take different routes to get where we eventually need to be, and Hill's is one of the more elaborate, given this late bloomer's years of searching and self-discovery. A book called *Thinking Body, Dancing Mind* is what helped lead him to seek out Dorfman.

"It was very eye opening because the year before, I was having some issues with trying to control breathing, control thoughts, trying to focus in on the moment," Hill says. "That was in '04. In '05, I came into spring training having read the book in the off season and I was completely focused, had a great spring and got called up a couple of months into the season. That was really what kind of kicked it off to me and opened my eyes to that process of thinking. That was the year I started conversing with Harvey a little bit, and he opened my eyes to a couple of different things as well."

In Pawtucket, in 2011, things were different for Hill because by then he was trapped in an unfamiliar place, pitching out of the bullpen. Unfamiliar places and uncomfortable situations are prime breeding grounds for the Little Man to appear. Now, something else important about the Little Man. This little devil isn't always saying *don't* or *can't* or feeding you negative images. He also leads you into the abyss of overthinking, of not trusting yourself or what you are doing. You think about your mechanics wondering, *Where's my arm slot*? You think about the pitch you just threw wondering, *What did I do wrong*? That focus siphons away important elements of your concentration and leads you away from the task at hand. For a pitcher who always has been a starter, going to the bullpen is like being grounded at your parents' house on the night of the homecoming dance. The beautiful people are all gathered at the cool place, while you're feeling lonely and left out.

I remember the first time I worked out of the bullpen in the big leagues. I had never pitched in relief, even while coming up in the Yankees system, but I'd been banished to the pen by Lou Piniella midway through the season. We were in Kansas City, and the first time the bullpen phone rang, my stomach felt like a twenty-pound anvil had just been shoved down my throat.

Danger zone right here. Rich was going through an already difficult transition, and he was an overthinking type of guy to begin with. So we worked to make sure he had a good mental plan before the game so that whatever inning he was called upon to pitch, he was in a calm, competitive state of mind and he was thinking the right things. What this would do, if everything worked as it should, was allow him to focus on that singular moment. Focus on his next pitch without his mind wandering. Throw each pitch with conviction, rather than throw it haphazardly while worrying about the next one. Trust that if he threw a pitch with conviction, it would be good enough. Building confidence with each good pitch, just as a mason builds a foundation one brick at a time.

"Stop thinking so much," I told him. "Go out and just compete."

In pure, old-school baseball terms, what Hill needed to do was to go out and deal.

"I was trying to go over things with self-imagery, look at things to get back into being more aggressive and attacking the strike zone with all of my pitches," Hill says. "There were some really good things he helped me with. Breathing. Things to stay in the moment.

"Trying to get into a good breathing program before the game, making sure that you're in a calm, competitive state before you go out and pitch so you basically are focusing in on the moment. Being able to focus on that pitch and not have your mind or your thoughts wander."

I put together an audio program so he could listen and reinforce important points where his breathing and imagery were concerned whenever he felt vulnerable.

"It's all these things you do over and over and over again," Hill says. "You make it a habit and it becomes part of your repertoire. It gives you a routine you can stay in, and you can revert back to it whether you're doing really well or not doing really well at all. It keeps you on the same plane."

The key is, when your mind is prepared, everything else follows. Imagery practice can help a player in all aspects of his performance. It begins with moving into a comfortable position, relaxing and focusing on your breathing. *"Take a long, slow breath, in through the nose, count to four, exhale slowly and fully through your mouth. Do it again, and feel your neck and shoulders relax . . . then again, and feel your jaw relax, and your face muscles. Now,"* I told Rich on the audio program I recorded for him, *"you're ready to begin your imagery practice."*

In your mind's eye, imagine yourself standing on the pitching rubber looking in at the catcher. Feel your cleats sinking into the pitching rubber and the dirt of the mound. Your arms are in front of your body, letter high. The ball and glove are in your hand together. As you hold the ball, you feel the seams as if you move the ball to get your fastball grip. You see the sign from the catcher and increase your attention to the catcher's mitt. Your mind is free, empty of any care or concern. Your focus is on throwing this pitch. Feel your right leg step back from the rubber as your left foot begins to slide into position in front of the rubber. You feel your foot settle against the pitcher rubber, crunching into the dirt in front of it, and your right leg comes around the front side of your body with your knee bent and leading the way. Your tempo is perfect. You're in a great balance position, arms and body gathered tall, ready to go to the plate. The break of your hands and the timing of your leg going up and then down, rotating toward the plate, are in sync. Your hands, which once were united in the glove, separate. You hold the ball firmly, but not too tight. Your arm begins its path out, down and then up. Your right shoulder remains closed with your elbow creating a line to your target, the plate. As your eyes remain fixed on the target, your head is still. Your legs and arms move around your body with perfect timing. Your right leg lands softly but firmly, creating a powerful base from which to leverage your pitch. Your arm accelerates forward with your hand on top of the baseball. You release the baseball with power, driving the pitch toward the plate on the perfect plane. Your body continues to finish its motion, your left leg comes around and gets you in position to field any ball that's hit back to you. Your body is in perfect position to deliver a competitive and assured pitch. You see the ball as it approaches your target and you know it is a quality pitch.

Now, take a moment to rewind this image and add some color to it. See the ball, which now is red, leave the catcher's mitt. Imagine it coming back to your hand in slow motion. Draw the ball back on the plane in which it traveled to the plate. Imagine the ball as it gets to the point where it's leaving your hand, and feel your fingers on top of the ball. Feel the ball as it touches the tips of your fingers, your hands on top of the ball. The ball settles comfortably into your hand and your arm moves backwards and rewinds from the release from the cocking phase, and your body rewinds also. Your left leg goes back to the pitching rubber. Your right leg goes back to being elevated. Your body slightly turns your knee up, your hands come back together again as you come into a balanced position. Now it rewinds even more to your side step, which initiated the whole move from where your windup was to begin with. Spend some time rewinding this, pulling all the details. Go slow.

He made good progress over ten appearances in Pawtucket and Boston summoned him to the bigs, where, over eight solid relief innings in nine appearances, Hill fanned twelve, looked promising . . .

and then it all came crashing down when his elbow gave out and he underwent Tommy John ligament replacement surgery in May. From there, you needed a GPS and a search engine to keep up with the poor guy. Though he came back with Boston in 2012, working a total of thirty-eight innings, the bouncing baseball led him to Cleveland in 2013, Boston, the Los Angeles Angels and the New York Yankees in 2014 and the Washington Nationals organization to start the 2015 season. Then he took a severe detour to the Long Island Ducks of the independent Atlantic League before re-signing with Boston, moving on to Oakland and, finally, landing with the Los Angeles Dodgers.

In the midst of this frequent-flier odyssey, I sat down with him in the Pawtucket dugout at old McCoy Stadium one day in 2014, the one year I worked for the Major League Baseball Players Association. As we chatted, Rich told me: "I really believe I can start again." My first thought was simple. *This guy is out of his mind!* At that moment, Hill was thirty-four and he'd bounced around as a reliever for the past five years. And now he's trying to find his way back to the big leagues as a starter? I tried to think rationally to give him some perspective on what this move would mean. I felt like major league teams only viewed him as a lefty specialist, given his age and lack of starting innings over recent years. Lefty specialists last forever, too, like Jesse Orosco and Javier López. "People need that," I told him. He just needed to commit to one arm slot, which he felt gave him the best chance to get lefties out. I told him I thought the only way for him to return to the majors as a starter would be for him to leave organized ball and go find a job as a starter in an independent league somewhere, and I thought that would be a risky career move.

So, what do I know, anyway?! That next summer, the Nationals released him early in the 2015 season and, sure enough, he wound up in Long Island with the Ducks. One summer later, Oakland took a flier on Hill and, finally, it was his time. Quack! Hill went 9-3 with a 2.25 ERA in fourteen starts, and the A's leveraged his peak by dealing him to the Dodgers at the July trade deadline. From there, Hill went 3-2 with a 1.86 ERA in six starts for Los Angeles in August and September, and then started and won Game 3 against the Cubs in the NLCS. I have never been happier for a player than I was for Rich when he signed a three-year, $48 million free-agent deal with the Dodgers in the winter of 2016–2017.

For Hill, who continues to incorporate his breathing and imagery program into his game today, it all begins long before he ever takes the mound on a given night.

"Your thoughts lead to your behaviors," he says. "If you can control and command your thought process, pre-pitch routines, make them the same every single time, if you've trained yourself enough to have that same routine, it really just continues to flow when you go out and pitch. There have been plenty of times I've been out there where I'm focusing on breathing, bringing your tempo down so you're not going too fast. Or, if you're going too slow, sometimes you need to pick it up."

From time to time, you hear pitching coaches and broadcasters talking about a pitcher's "tempo." One component of a successful night on the mound is working at a good tempo: not too fast, but not too slow. A productive pace that keeps the pitcher and catcher working together in harmony, keeps the pitcher in a good rhythm and keeps the fielders alert and on their toes. But this does not happen magically, or by accident.

"For anybody in any field, if you can have that association where you can relate to [a mentor] in that particular field, I think it's very important," Hill says. "And Tewks brings something you can't learn in school unless you actually go through it and do it. And he did.

"Baseball seems like it's simple on the outside. And sometimes we make it too complicated, too, and that's why we need to slow things down and get back into the moment."

If there is any doubt in any given moment, like Miller, Hill has become very adept at redirecting that moment. Two lefties in their right minds. Breathe in. Breathe out. And go to an anchor statement, just as others reach for the rosin bag on the mound.

This pitch, with trust, confidence and conviction.

11

Putting on the Riz

Inside of Anthony Rizzo's computer are the guts of the thoughts he takes with him each trip into the on-deck circle and then into the batter's box. These guts come packaged one by one, eleven tracks in all, downloaded from an audio program left over from his days as a teenager in the Boston Red Sox organization. Great thing about this tool kit is, it's transferrable. Wherever he goes, in whichever city he calls home, it's just a click or two away.

It's been with him now through three All-Star Game appearances, two top-five National League Most Valuable Player finishes (fourth in the voting both in 2015 and 2016), one Gold Glove (2016), one

Silver Slugger (2016) and, of course, one Chicago Cubs World Series title (2016). You may have heard.

"It's all mental," Rizzo says of his program, which beams like a lighthouse guiding him home when things get foggy. "It's about visualizing, positive self-talk, performance anchor statements that guide you through at-bats. Breathing. You're talking good thoughts to yourself. 'I am a good hitter. I see the ball right out of the pitcher's hand.' And then repeat it two or three times. 'When I get into the box, I am the best player.'"

One of the things I routinely do while coaching mental skills is produce audio programs that players easily can download to their iPhones. Track by track, the idea is to give them, or help remind them of, performance cues. From Jon Lester to Rizzo to Andrew Miller to Rich Hill, as the kids develop into veterans, so many tell me these programs remain current and are vital to them today.

For Rizzo, I personalized the program and sandwiched an inspirational song of his choosing between tracks pertaining to breathing, self-talk, perception and anchor statements. *See the ball, hit the ball.* There is a second program, eleven tracks in all, that I produced for young hitters at the time Rizzo was coming up in the Boston organization that expands on those tenets and moves into urgency, fairness, goals, expectations, relaxation, visualization and performance anchor statements.

Rizzo's personalized program is sort of a greatest-hits package of the longer, eleven-track program, the key points and touchstone phrases boiled down. As Anthony says, those early years, when a player is in the eighteen- to twenty-two-year-old range, are some of the most important of his life. Developing good habits and learning important concepts at that stage will last a lifetime.

"I listen to his stuff even now," Rizzo says. "When I get into a rut, I'll throw on tracks one through eleven, put it on repeat and fall asleep listening to it.

"It locks you in. Repeating things. When you hear positive self-talk, that's what it's all about. This game's all mental. Everyone at this level in the big leagues has always been the best on his teams his entire life. So the only thing that's separating us, or stopping us, is between the ears."

For a hitter, that space can clog up frequently, like pedestrian traffic on Chicago's Rush Street on a Saturday night. Not only must he prepare to face a different starting pitcher with unique challenges every single night—from Clayton Kershaw's deception to Chris Sale's angles to Noah Syndergaard's intimidation to the rookie he hasn't seen yet and must break down quickly—but in today's game, bullpen doors swing open and deliver stacks of relievers nightly as if by assembly line. From breaking balls to sliders to high fastballs to bad luck to awful umpires' calls to agents' suggestions as to how this all correlates with his next contract, there is much to assimilate, and quickly. One beautiful thing about all of today's plush, modern ballparks is that they come equipped with indoor batting cages, and almost every team has added an assistant hitting coach to help the main hitting coach, which means hitters always have access to more batting practice, which can be a good thing . . . until they feel obligated to take more and more BP, especially because their teammates are doing it, and then there's all of that video to watch on the clubhouse hitters, which can be helpful . . . to a point . . . until all of these things blend together and overwhelm and hitters begin overthinking and descend into the quicksand of paralysis by analysis.

There is so much going on in that sixty-foot, six-inch space between the mound and the plate that it isn't only the fiery, intimidating pitchers like a Bumgarner or a Nolan Ryan who can cross the wires between a hitter's ears. Even an unintimidating guy like me who accidentally hits a batter in the head during a minor league game can do it. It was during a Double-A game when I hit Andrés Galarraga, who would become a fearsome slugger for the Montreal

Expos. It was purely and unequivocally unintentional. But when we both landed in the majors and he hit just .158 (6 for 38) against me with a .179 on-base percentage, two homers and three RBIs in thirty-nine plate appearances, I chalked part of it up to the fact that he probably never forgot that minor league incident. Especially when he started 0 for 11 against me in the majors. Maybe it helped me have some success by giving him something extra to think about.

That's the purpose of pitching inside: to plant thoughts in the heads of hitters that perhaps would never get there otherwise. Yes, a ball can be a weapon and, unfortunately, hitters do get hit by pitches. I am completely comfortable in saying that the majority of times batters are hit, it's accidental. It is a very, very thin line. To survive, pitchers must work inside. They cannot give the inner half of the plate to a hitter, otherwise, it is career suicide. Yet, pitchers do lose command of fastballs, they throw sloppy curveballs that don't break, or sliders that break too much, and next thing you know, *thunk!* The horsehide is burrowing its way into the batter's flesh. In the most extreme cases, it is horrifying, as when Giancarlo Stanton was hit in the face in 2014 by a Mike Fiers fastball and blood poured from his mouth right there at home plate, or when Dickie Thon was hit in the face in 1984 by a Mike Torrez fastball. Stanton suffered multiple facial fractures and dental damage. Thon suffered a broken left orbital bone, battled vision problems for the rest of his career and never developed into the player the industry thought he would become.

There are times, of course, when a batter is hit purely as an act of retaliation, usually based on old-school unwritten rules. You hit my guy, so now I've got to hit your guy. Or if a batter pimps a home run, or if a rival baserunner bowls over your catcher or takes out your middle infielder at second base. In cases like that, you get them back and batters often are expecting it (not that it prevents some from charging the mound anyway!).

Problems, however, come from a variety of angles. Pitchers gradually have stopped pitching inside in today's game—among other things, aluminum bats take that edge away when they're young, so they really don't grow up practicing how to pitch inside without hitting a batter. Pitchers are throwing more breaking balls and that, combined with the hitters not being afraid of the ball (because they're not getting pitched inside as much), causes many hitters to lean out over the plate because they are looking for pitches on the outer half more often. As a result, the pitch inside looks *really* inside, and hitters take offense to this and it creates emotions that easily can escalate. Hitters wear arm guards for protection, but that allows the hitter to be comfortable in the box (if it sounds like there may be a bit of resentment here from my view as a former pitcher ... guilty!).

So toss all of this into the gumbo of real-time actions and reactions, and often you reach a point where if the need arises to hit a batter, many pitchers don't know how to do it on purpose. Back to the unwritten rules of the game. One of the chief ones is this: If a pitcher needs to do it, hit the batter below the waist. I loved to pitch Hall of Famer Craig Biggio inside, and getting hit by a pitch was one of his chief offensive weapons. He was drilled 285 times in his career, second all-time to Hughie Jennings (287). Ouch! So one time, a pitch got away from me and went up and in. From the plate, Biggio hollered at me: "You can pitch inside, but don't throw at my head!" It was purely accidental on my part, but point taken. Biggio was right, and the devastation that happened to Stanton, Thon and many others is a stark reminder. Boston's Matt Barnes is a good kid, but his buzzing of the tower of Baltimore's Manny Machado in retaliation for Machado's slide into Dustin Pedroia in 2016 was unacceptable.

Obviously, the head is the most dangerous place to get hit, and when it happens, nobody knows how a player will come back. So much depends on the player's makeup—some adjust back quite well, but others never can seem to find their groove again. From the batter's box, this is just the tip of the pitching iceberg as a hitter assimilates everything he knows about the pitcher he is facing: previous history against him, that pitcher's tendencies, scouting reports, what's already happened in today's game, the situation—score, inning, outs and, as the at-bat proceeds, the count. So much information.

Eliminating so many of these extraneous thoughts is crucial at the plate, and one way I think is beneficial toward doing so is to give the hitter something to listen to.

Rizzo was Boston's sixth-round pick in 2007. That was the year I produced the mental skills audio program and, like college freshmen receiving their orientation packets, Rizzo was in the first "class" in the Red Sox organization to receive my production. That he still refers to it to keep himself on track today, a full decade later, is beyond cool. Here is a brief overview.

TRACK 1: An overall introduction to making the choice to sharpen your mental skills and, believe me, this is a choice. Pure and simple. It is a choice many players don't make, instead choosing to spend most of their time on physical and fundamental areas and neglecting how important the mind is when it comes to performance. Mistake. Athletes face choices every day that affect their performance: how much sleep they get, what they eat, what they think about and how they react to things out of their control (like poor playing conditions, or what they think is a bad call by the umpire). Making the choice to get angry leads to frustration, and when an athlete is frustrated he often dwells on failure, loses confidence, and that leads to focusing on the problem rather than on the solution. Being good every day is difficult, and dealing with your performance when things are not going well—which most assuredly will happen more often than a player would like; it's a looooong season—well, there's a name for that: mental toughness.

TRACK 2: *Perception, Fairness and Urgency.* Part of what Rizzo is referring to when he talks about what can clog things up between a player's ears is perception, which is how each one of us views something specific. In both baseball and in life, events are perceived differently by each of us. Is the glass half empty or half full? Some hitters cannot wait to come to the plate to hit with runners in scoring position. For others, that situation produces more anxiety than a roomful of rocking chairs for a long-tailed cat. Part of what colors perception is fairness. How often have all of us in our lifetimes been dumped, duped, rejected, neglected, overlooked or undersold? So often that we've all been consoled by, and accept, family members and friends telling us: "Life isn't always fair." Now, here's another question: Is baseball fair? Hitters watch scorching liners *thwack* into waiting gloves all the time, and when it happens over a few games, players often will revert to *It's not fair! Why does this happen to me?* Let's circle back for a moment. Life, as you recall from a few sentences ago, is not fair. Baseball is a part of life. Therefore, baseball is not fair. The only thing we know for sure about pegging something as "not fair" is this: that response does not change a single thing. It only leads to more frustration, which often leads to increased effort level, which often leads to diminishing returns. Dwelling on it only makes the issue worse. Once the ball leaves the hitter's bat, there is nothing he can do about it. Same thing for a pitcher. Once the ball leaves his hand, the result is out of his control. How a player handles unfairness is similar to his decision about how much work he applies toward mental skills. It's a choice.

Finally, perception and fairness lead to urgency, which can either be constructive or destructive. Naturally, most players have a sense of urgency regarding their careers, which leads them to do the work necessary to keep moving forward. But when that urgency leads to a false sense of perception that makes a player believe "I've got to do (fill in the blank) *now,*" that's where things quickly can turn destructive. This again often is a response to a perceived, threatening event. Runners on second and third, nobody out and the hitter thinking, *I've got to get these runners in now!* Hitter leading off an inning after striking out with the bases loaded last time up thinking, *I looked so bad last time, I have to show these guys I'm better than that right here!* Or, the hitter comes to the plate knowing he's 0 for his last 10 and carrying the weight of the world on his shoulders, completely ignoring the context that up until now, he's had a very solid year and that his organization is judging him on that, not solely on his last 10 plate appearances. No matter. He is pressing, perceiving that his situation is far more dire than it really is. Well, whether you're 0 for your last 10 or 10 for your last 10, a hitter's job is exactly the same every time. Focus on one thing, and one thing only, and that is "seeing the ball." Then, when it is time, focus on the pitch after that. A false sense of urgency leads to muscles tightening up and to attempting to do more than you're capable of doing.

Once, I was working with a player in his hotel room, of all places, talking things out. I threw a pillow at him, and then another. And then another. There he was on the bed, covered in pillows, and I told him: "That's the baggage you're carrying. We all carry baggage, but we cannot let it get too heavy, and we've got to be smart about unloading it." I instructed him: "Toss away one of the pillows. Now, toss away another one. This is you unloading that baggage you're carrying. As you toss it away, visualize how much freer you are without those pillows covering you."

Instead of tightening up, players must find ways to lighten up. They don't say "Work ball!" to start; they say "Play ball!" This is a game. Though it admittedly gets more and more difficult as you climb that career ladder, players must find ways to take the same viewpoint as when they were in Little League and high school and have fun. Joyful players are better players, and one way I try to encourage this is through levity.

Now, maybe I'm no Steve Martin or Louis C.K., but laughter can rank right there with a cortisone shot in the medicine department, and I've been known to practice what I preach in terms of looking for opportunities to help others lighten up. One scorching-hot July day in 2013 when the Portland Sea Dogs, Boston's Class AA team, had lost eight in a row, I showed up to deliver a motivational speech to the boys while wearing a chipmunk costume. Laura had given it to me for Christmas one year after a local costume shop closed. She and our daughter, Jenna, share Halloween birthdays, which makes for an enormous celebration in our house, and I had rented that outfit enough that Laura figured she should just buy it. So there I was in Portland, wearing a giant, smiling chipmunk head, hollering at the Sea Dogs to "go out and kick some ass!" Alas, they lost that night . . . but snapped their losing streak the next night when Red Sox pitcher Matt Barnes struck out ten over seven innings. Surely, with the words of the chipmunk motivating him, right Matt?

TRACK 3: *Goals and Expectations.* Almost everyone sets goals. Generally speaking, of course, goals can be healthy and productive. But when we set unrealistic goals, the opposite is true. Then, they become an impediment to achievement because they can lead to too much self-induced, paralyzing pressure. Baseball players, of course, are measured by numbers. Batting average. ERA. Home runs. RBIs. Strikeouts. Wins and losses. That's all fine long term, but remember, once the ball leaves the bat, the hitter essentially is helpless. That's why, in baseball, "process" goals are the best kind of goals. Example: For a hitter, instead of picking a singular number of home runs or batting average, focus on the daily routine that you *can* control; things like tee work, pre-at-bat routine, on-deck routine, at-the-plate routine. Seeing the baseball. Better relaxation. Better thoughts when you come to the plate. A process that clears your mind, essentially, and allows that uncluttered mind freedom to focus solely on seeing the ball.

This is where a refined sense of self-awareness becomes an important tool. Several years ago, I was working with a minor league third baseman who was coming along nicely and was well thought of by the organization when, suddenly, he began obsessing on the need to develop more power.

"Who in the organization told you that you needed to do this?" I asked, a bit perplexed.

"Well, um, nobody," he confided. "But I'm a corner infielder so I know I need to start hitting home runs."

This, even though most big-league talent evaluators will tell you that power is among the last tools to develop at the major league level. In this instance, the player created an unrealistic expectation largely because of his false perception regarding what *he* believed he needed to do to get to the big leagues.

The best goals are process goals, which, in layman's language means "how to get there" goals, and they are important because they are controllable. Outcome goals are not controllable, and putting too much focus on them can be detrimental to a player's overall performance because oftentimes outcome goals are not realistically attainable. And when they are not achieved, a player loses some confidence and feels discouraged and frustrated. This results in continued poor performance, which only deepens the despair of the player until finally he stops caring or trying, and then begins to perform well again. Why? Because he let go of focusing on the outcomes and *accepted* what he can and cannot control.

Acceptance is a part of a process goal that cannot be emphasized enough. Dorfman regularly asked players three questions to help them reach a rational understanding of what just happened in order to help them redirect their thinking. Instead of allowing them to focus on the simple thought *I made an out, I feel bad*, he put three questions before them. What were you trying to do? (for example, move the runner to second base by hitting the ball to the right side of the field). What went wrong, if anything? (the hitter pulled the ball to shortstop and didn't advance the runner because he swung at an off-speed pitch that had him in front of the ball, resulting in a ground ball to shortstop). What will you do better next time? (next time, in that same situation, I will not swing at a breaking ball).

This is such a brilliant exercise for players who may fall short of a goal or objective. I use it all the time when I play golf. By asking yourself these questions, you identify your goal (intent), you evaluate what went wrong (if anything, because sometimes you do everything correctly and still don't achieve your desired goal) and, lastly, by phrasing step three "next time, I'll . . ." you are moving on from what happened and you already are creating a positive expectation of what you will do in the same situation in the future.

And, not stated here, Are you really being good to yourself? That is far more productive than throwing up your hands and beating yourself up over the unsuccessful outcome.

TRACK 4: *Positive Self-Talk.* This is where the Little Man appears, that voice that worms into your head like a termite with negative thoughts, working to break down positive self-talk by finding cracks in your mental toughness. It is vital to let that thought pass, like a cloud in the sky, and then refocus on the anchor statement and the task at hand. Once a player controls the Little Man, he rapidly will find that he's reacting to situations and games with new confidence.

TRACK 5: *Breathing and Relaxation.* The ultimate challenge for a professional athlete is to find the proper combination of the physical and mental places that will produce the ultimate performance state. And this begins with the ability to utilize their breath properly. This will greatly increase the chances of their gaining control of the situation rather than the situation controlling them. How many times have you heard a coach or a broadcaster say that the great athletes are able to slow the game down? Not everyone can slow the game down to the level of, say, a Larry Bird or, yes, an Anthony Rizzo, but controlled breathing by far is your best chance to slow it down to a manageable level.

TRACK 6: *Introduction to Visualization.* There is so much downtime in this game—on flights, on bus rides, in the clubhouse in the hours leading up to game time—so why not make it productive? Visualization can be performed and mastered in those lazy moments that fall under that "time management" umbrella. It starts simply with thinking about what you want to mentally rehearse. A nice, balanced swing? A perfect follow-through on a swing? Crushing a slider? Hitting with men on base? Once you've got a plan, find a comfortable place where you can either sit down or lie down, and begin by taking a few breaths. Notice a pattern here? Yes, everything starts with proper breathing. The best visualization engages each sense. See the pitcher, and visualize details. The color of his uniform. The batter's eye background. Hear your music, and the PA announcer saying your name as you're coming to the plate. Feel yourself walking to the plate, stepping in and digging a nice, comfortable spot in the batter's box. Smell the fresh air, and the hot dogs from the concessions. Finally, start the projector. Picture yourself drilling pitch after pitch up the middle, swing balanced, follow-through perfect. Or, is it one pitch you want to hit? Use your free time properly, and there will be moments in the game that will feel very much like you've already been there before. Because you have.

TRACK 7: *Guided Imagery.* A continuation of track 6, but far, far more specific. This is a guided tour through the entire imagery process, highly detailed, from start to finish.

TRACK 8: *Introduction to Performance Anchors* describes what anchor statements are and their many uses. We explored their usage with Andrew Miller in chapter 10; how they can reframe negative thoughts and help a player focus during anxious situations before or during a game.

TRACK 9: *Performance Anchor Statements.* In which I use my most soothing, late-night FM deejay voice to repeat various specific examples of anchor statements that players hopefully will co-opt and make their own. And "repeat" is a key word here. Each example, I repeat three times, slowly. *I am aggressive and under control . . . My motions are smooth . . . My swing is effortless and easy . . . I like hitting with men on base . . . I swing at pitches in my zone. . . . I am a good hitter.*

TRACK 10: *What Is the Ultimate Task of a Hitter?* Is it to hit the ball hard somewhere? Make solid contact? Reach base via a hit or walk? All true, and all relevant to the art of hitting. But *seeing* the baseball first and foremost is the ultimate task. As Hall of Famer Ted Williams said, "When you are concentrating on getting a hit, you don't see the ball well. But when you concentrate on seeing the ball, you hit it well. And then the hits take care of themselves." A hitter could have the best, most perfect mechanics in the world, but if I blindfolded him, he would be helpless. How many times have you heard a hot hitter say he's "seeing the ball well right now"? For those hitters, the baseball looks "like a beach ball." And when a hitter isn't hitting, it's the opposite. You will hear him say, "I'm not seeing the ball right now." For those hitters, the baseball looks like a red peanut M&M. Seeing the ball begins with a broad external focus. When that hitter is in the on-deck circle, he thinks about what situation he will be presented with when he comes to the plate and what needs to be done when he steps in. Is it moving the runner over? A hit-and-run? A fly ball? Putting down a bunt? Once at the plate, the hitter changes to a narrow, internal focus when he sees the pitcher delivering the pitch. The goal is to see the ball as quickly as you can to recognize the spin and pitch location and, then, hit it.

TRACK 11: *Hitter's Performance Checklist.* This is something a hitter can revisit to make sure he is doing everything he can do. It is both physical *and* mental preparation. Is he getting his rest? Doing his weight work? Cage work? Keeping the same routine? Same batting practice routine pregame? Breathing? Accepting things out of his control? How's the concentration? Is he seeing the ball? Is he controlling his emotions, or are feelings getting in the way? Is he focusing on the task at hand? Is he beating himself up after bad at-bats? How about the body language? Is it positive and productive? Is the hitter acting with confidence? There is an old saying, "Fake it to make it." Self-doubt is normal, but exceptional people and exceptional players do not give in to it. Stick with the process and the results will come. You have great ability, now get out of its way and let it play! Perhaps the biggest opponent you'll ever have is yourself—and for many of us, that's true on the field *and* off of it.

For Rizzo, the preparation for each plate appearance starts at the same place every time.

"You're always breathing," he says. "When stuff starts to speed up on you, you have to slow it down. And the best way to slow it down is by breathing [properly]. Before the game, everyone gets all hyped up. For me personally, I try to stay in the zone and slow everything down and never get overhyped. I try and slow things down no matter what. Obviously, the emotions get to you, but you try to stay one level at all times."

As he says, "Breathing is the biggest thing. Get your breath. Slow your heart rate down. When you do that, you can start controlling your body a little bit more."

Charting Rizzo's development over the past decade, from a young, unsure prospect in Boston and San Diego to confident All-Star in Chicago, also is a study in some of the issues and solutions contained in that audio program. Take urgency, some of which Rizzo undoubtedly felt when he debuted with the Padres at twenty-one late in 2011 and hit .141 over 153 plate appearances in forty-nine games. Younger players, of course, are more susceptible to feeling vulnerable, rather than confident, in threatening situations. When I was a rookie with the Yankees, White Sox catcher Carlton Fisk, who would wind up in Cooperstown, reached first base in the middle innings of a close game. Looking in for the sign from my catcher, I quickly wheeled and threw over to first base, twice. The issue? Both times, Fisk was still standing on the base without even having taken a lead! I was overanxious and uncomfortable because Fisk was on first base and, therefore, he might score. As I got older and gained experience, I came to realize that there always would be baserunners, umpires always would miss calls, and fielders behind me occasionally would boot a ground ball. It seemed like there would be two or three situations each game in which I would have to work out of a perceived "threatening" situation.

As Rizzo got older and gained experience, he finished tenth in NL MVP voting in 2014 and then fourth in the voting in each of the next two years. At twenty-five in 2015, he led the NL in both games played (160) and plate appearances (701). At twenty-six in 2016, he had emerged as one of the veteran leaders of that very young Cubs title team. He had learned to breathe, visualize and slow things down, which, of course, is the best line of defense to drain the air out of that sense-of-urgency bubble. As Ravizza started preaching to players in the 1980s, one of the keys to performing is becoming "comfortable with feeling uncomfortable."

I remember meeting Anthony when he was eighteen at the old Red Sox spring training complex on Edison Avenue in Fort Myers. I was at Instructional League that year becoming acquainted with the young players in the organization. Now, I'm no scout, but the first time I saw Riz take batting practice, I knew this guy had a big-league swing. He's changed it some over the years but, as we all know, this guy can *hit*. I found that he was a very real and genuinely nice kid. It was no surprise, based on the way he carried himself, that he came from a close-knit family. It showed. Anthony is a very driven athlete. I remember Riz calling me while he was playing for Salem, in High

Class A ball, complaining about not being able to get more than one hit in a game over the course of a week. I remember thinking, *Is he serious?* Most players complain about not getting any hits in a game. Riz was looking for more. I wasn't surprised when Theo Epstein and the Cubs found a way to obtain him from the Padres in 2012, just two years after Theo had traded him there in the Adrian Gonzalez deal before Epstein left Boston. I always thought the Red Sox had their first baseman for the next several years when Rizzo was there; he was just a year or two away.

Boston, San Diego, Chicago . . . wherever he would wind up, his success is not surprising to me because, aside from his obvious physical skills, he has perspective on both life and baseball. And the mental skills techniques that Rizzo first devoured at eighteen served him just as expertly when he emerged as one of the pillars of Chicago manager Joe Maddon's clubhouse, helping the Cubs win a World Series. As a perennial All-Star now, there is no specific situation in each game in which Rizzo applies these techniques, simply because they have become a part of who he is and what he does. He is *always* applying them.

"Whenever you get nervous in the on-deck circle, which I get nervous all the time, you just do it," he says.

Rizzo then takes that breathing with him to the plate, calmer than when he stepped into the on-deck circle, and the routine has become so ingrained for him that he's stumped when he's asked to review his controlled breathing patterns once he digs into the batter's box.

"I don't know, I just do it," he says. "Take deep breaths. Kind of lock in on what the pitcher's got, his approach, my approach, and stick with it. Another thing Tewks is big on is one pitch at a time. It's so cliché, but it's true. You take it one pitch at a time. One at-bat at a time. And you really don't have to worry about anything else. You'll be all right.

"When you breathe, you can do everything. Visualize. You can really slow it down, and visualization is as important as breathing. You've gotta control your thoughts. The deeper the breath you take, the more you breathe, the more you're focused on your breathing instead of why did I suck there? Why am I doing so well? Sometimes, you overanalyze it. Why am I doing so well? Just go with it."

In the fifth inning of Game 7 of the '16 World Series, with the Cubs leading Cleveland in front of a sold-out Progressive Field, the largest national television audience for a baseball game in a quarter of a century, and with the tension level at Defcon 1, Rizzo and his beloved teammate David Ross, miked for the Fox cameras, shared some of this with the entire country. Rizzo stepped up next to Ross at the Cubs' dugout railing, and as broadcast by Fox, this is how their highly entertaining conversation went, with film buff Rizzo eventually going all Ron Burgundy from *Anchorman*:

RIZZO: "I can't control myself right now. I'm trying my best."
ROSS: "It's understandably so, buddy."
RIZZO: "I'm emotional."
ROSS: "I hear ya."
RIZZO: "I'm an emotional wreck."
ROSS: "Well, it's only going to get worse. Just continue to breathe. That's all you can do, buddy. It's only going to get worse."
RIZZO: "I'm in a glass case of emotion right now."
ROSS: "Wait until the ninth with this three-run lead."

Rizzo, who has become quite an endearing character in the game, was playing up the moment with humor and exaggeration. As he said of that exchange in the spring of 2017: "We always mess around in the dugout, it's Game 7, we're coming off four weeks of the most intense, fire-to-the-nose baseball there is, that was just messing around–slash-serious, knowing every pitch is worth so much. But in the field and at-bat, you just let the game take over."

Within the sublime entertainment, in the midst of the pressure and jangly nerves, though, the moment was instructive because Grandpa Rossy, the wise ol' veteran knew that even in "a glass case of emotion" produced by a World Series, rising to the moment begins with a conscious effort to focus on breathing.

And for Rizzo, breathing and visualization exercises continue to serve as an important part of his daily routine. Even, as he says, when he sometimes doesn't always recognize he's doing it. "When the stuff hits the fan, you've got to get back to the basics," Rizzo says.

And when that happens, the man who carried the club's first World Series trophy in 108 years from center field back into the infield during the Cubs' championship banner–raising ceremony at their 2017 home opener, the man who emotionally hoisted the trophy high in the air over his head as the roar of another sellout Wrigley Field crowd washed over him, settles snugly into his bed, clicks play and falls asleep listening as tracks one through eleven remind him of where he needs to be when he awakens tomorrow morning.

12

Pitchology

As Jon Lester remembers it, the noise surrounding Fenway Park before Games 1 and 5 of the 2013 World Series was deafening. Inside Boston's man-made "sleep room" in the Red Sox's clubhouse, however, the scene was so peaceful as to induce the very thing the space was named for. Before a couple of the biggest games of his life, listening on his iPod to the imagery program I created for him, St. Louis's skilled leadoff hitter Matt Carpenter waiting not too far off in the distance, Lester's breathing melted into ... *zzzz* ... *zzz* ... *ZZZZ*.

The confusion that confounded Lester that midseason in Oakland ever so slowly had evaporated. The frustration he'd been experiencing receded. As he settled into this new pregame breathing and imagery routine during the season's second half, he discovered that, better than ever before, he was able to organize his thoughts and control his mind. Breakthrough. In the second half of that summer, Lester chopped his ERA by two runs per game, from 4.58 pre–All-Star Game to 2.57 post. He located a consistency he knew he had within him but had been unable to harness. Following easily the worst year-and-a-half stretch of his career, the 2012 season and the first half of 2013—in '12, his twenty-five home runs allowed still stand as a career high—Lester regained both his balance and his edge.

He established himself that fall as an October anchor, something he would carry forward into his years with the Cubs, by going 4-1 with a 1.56 ERA, twenty-nine strikeouts and just eight walks in five postseason starts that autumn to lead the Red Sox to another World Series victory.

From that leather couch in the small office in the visitors' clubhouse in Oakland to the tiny, 145-square-foot sleep room the Red Sox created upstairs in their clubhouse in '13, at the recommendation of a sleep specialist who consulted with the team, Lester turned things around one deep, focused and purposeful breath at a time.

Using that All-Star break to decompress at his home in Georgia, Lester decided that the imagery drill I led him through in Oakland could be a valuable tool. Especially because there were moments in the game that next night during which he felt like he already had pitched. Sort of like those moments you probably have from time to time that are mysteriously familiar because you feel you already were there in a dream. Except, this was no dream. Upon returning from the break, Lester phoned and asked, "What else do you have? Where can we take this?" What we settled on was a multipart program that Lester continues to tap into today.

Typically, two hours or so before a 7:05 P.M. start, Lester will get his ankles taped and go into a meeting with his catcher and pitching coach to review that night's opposing lineup. Then, between 5:30

and 6:00, he will carve out some alone time to work on concentration grids, and then lie down and hit play on the imagery program on his smartphone.

The concentration grids look like crossword puzzles, with jumbled-up numbers from 00 through 99. They are index-card sized, each number is in a small box and the numbers are in different, random orders on each card. The exercise is designed to help a person increase and sharpen his focus, and each drill is timed, usually thirty seconds or sixty seconds. When a card is finished, he flips to the next card, and this drill also is timed. The numbers on that card could be in the same order as the previous card, or totally (and randomly) different. The numbers stay the same, 00 through 99.

To accompany these grids, I made Jon another audio program that leads him through the process of focusing. There are five or six one-minute exercises, each with different instructions. For example, on grid no. 1, starting at 00, going up by two, see how many numbers you can find (00, 02, 04, 06 and so on). After one minute on the audio, I say, "Stop." Then, prepare for grid no. 2. One minute later, stop.

Where it changes is with grid nos. 5 and 6. There, I added background noises designed to frequently interrupt Jon's focus. "Get ready for grid no. 5, this time with distractions. Count up by five. Ready . . . go." Now, as he searches for the numbers, he hears horns, trains and other noises intermittently in his earbuds. Same with grid no. 6. And within this, the numbers change and so do the instructions—maybe now he counts backwards from ninety-nine by three.

"I always had a problem, and I still have a problem, which is, I get too far ahead of myself," Lester says, speaking of the nightly battle he wages with himself on the mound. "So in the game, say you get a guy 0 and 1, instead of worrying about that pitch, the second pitch of the at-bat, I'm going, 'Okay, I'm going to get strike two, then I'm going to do this.' Instead of going, 'It's 0 and 1, what am I going to do here? What pitch am I going to focus on here?' and do that as opposed to worry about the pitch after that or the pitch after that. Or a pitch prior to that that hurt me, that I didn't get the call on, something like that."

The point of all of this was very specific: To pull Lester's mind away from whatever was going on in his day and slowly shift it into game mode, to a point where he had a singular, pitch-by-pitch focus. Just like locating each number on the grid, one number at a time, it's one pitch at a time. I felt that by changing the task of finding the numbers—up or down—it would engage his mind to really focus on his task that night. And by creating an audio, Jon could do this anytime he wanted, at home, on the road, anytime, anyplace.

So often, you hear about the game speeding up on players. This is one tactic to slow it back down. Focus on the moment in front of you, not on the moment you will face one minute from now, or three minutes from now, or who knows how long from now.

"It really simplifies things, taking it one pitch at a time," Lester says. "It's almost like a game within a game. *I want to win this game. I want to win this pitch.* With these cards, you go 00, okay, now you're looking for 02. Human instinct is, you find 04 while you're looking so you say, 'I'll remember where that's at while I'm looking for 02.' So now I'm worried about where that third pitch is going instead of trying to execute the second pitch, worrying about where that's going.

"So 04 is the third pitch, for example. You're not trying to focus on 04. You're looking for 02, 02, 02 . . . Okay, now the third pitch: 04, where's 04?"

As he changed his landscape one start at a time in the second half of '13, when Lester finished with the concentration grids, he disappeared upstairs into the sleep room (when the team was home), nestled into bed, popped in his earbuds and clicked play on the audio program leading him through his imagery drill. In the quiet of the early evening, first pitch creeping close enough to reach out and touch, he would close his eyes and listen as my voice led him through different pitches in different situations: *Okay, the count is 0 and 2, right-handed hitter, fastball hitter, your pitch is a perfect fastball down and away . . . and the umpire balls it. It should have been a strike. But he balls it. So now, instead of a strikeout, the count is 1 and 2. This is what you should do next. This is how you should react . . .*

"I think it's about a thirteen-minute thing, and I'm usually in for twenty or thirty minutes and end up falling asleep," Lester says. "So I set an alarm. And that's kind of what he wants you to do, relax. It all starts with relaxing and breathing, then the program walks into the game and goes from there."

Now, slow your own breathing, close your eyes and visualize this: *Game 1 of the World Series, October 23, 2013, and 38,345 are stuffing Fenway Park, with millions upon millions more fans watching on television.* And within ninety minutes or so of his first pitch, Lester literally sets an alarm to wake him as he drifts off in the quiet of the sleep room while visualizing his pitches to Carpenter, Carlos Beltrán and Matt Holliday, the first three Cardinals hitters coming to the plate in the first inning. From our beginnings that July, yep, I'd say Lester had moved from a skeptic to becoming fully invested in the benefits of what a good mental skills program can do to boost performance.

Beginning immediately after that All-Star break in 2013, in his first two starts Jon seized control of his season and took a sharp turn back in the direction of the pitcher he knew he again could be. Against a Tampa Bay club that would finish 92-71 and secure an American League wild-card playoff slot that autumn, he surrendered just two earned runs and seven hits in 6.1 innings during a 6-2 win. Then he fired seven shutout, four-hit innings in Camden Yards against a strong Baltimore team that would finish 85-77. Back in the Bay Area on August 19, he was spectacular over 8.1 innings in San Francisco's beautiful AT&T Park, holding the Giants to six hits in a 7-0 victory. And down the stretch in September, over five starts he went 3-0 with a 2.57 ERA, striking out thirty-two against only seven walks.

Watching it all come together for Jon that summer was a sight to behold, not only for all of Red Sox Nation, of course, but especially from my small corner of that universe. Anytime a player is engaged in his work and feels that in some way I may have helped him perform better, well, of course that always feels good. But what I remember most about his turnaround during that '13 season isn't what he did or didn't do on the mound. It simply is the many conversations we had during the week. I would regularly check in with him to see how his new program was going, and whether there was anything he wanted to discuss. Much of the time, our conversations weren't even about baseball. We would talk about his kids, or the building project at his ranch in Georgia or about how far I *didn't* hit the golf ball. (Often, he helpfully suggested that I hit from the ladies' tees, which made me think that if I weren't such a nice guy, I could review his guitar playing for him! Not long ago I texted him, bragging that he should have seen one of my drives, and he shot right back that he was sure it couldn't have been more than two hundred yards.)

Even today, I can still hear him calling out: "Tewks, get back here!" on the Red Sox charter flights to Detroit and St. Louis that postseason, a summons for me to join the boys in the back of the plane to have a drink and engage in memorable sessions in which we simply shot the breeze with John Lackey, Jake Peavy and others who were playing poker, talking about how we were going to "win this thing."

To "win this thing," after we threaded our way through a rugged Detroit team featuring Justin Verlander and Max Scherzer atop the rotation in the AL Championship Series—and thanks in no small part to series MVP David Ortiz (whose epic two-out, eighth-inning, Game 2 grand slam against Joaquín Benoit sent Torii Hunter tumbling upside down over the outfield wall and immediately went viral)—we were going to have to plow through a St. Louis team that produced the best record in the National League at 97-65.

And facing Lester in Game 1 would be Adam Wainwright, who was absolutely dominant that summer, going 19-9 with a 2.34 ERA in 241.2 innings over thirty-four starts. He led the NL in wins, starts, innings pitched and batters faced (956). At thirty-one and with a curveball so sharp it defied conventional geometry, Wainwright was at the peak of his powers and, not long after that World Series, would finish second in the NL Cy Young voting to Clayton Kershaw of the Los Angeles Dodgers. Even though Lester had found his groove in the second half, the pundits all viewed Wainwright as the heavy favorite as the curtain opened on the Fall Classic.

All Lester did was emerge from that sleep room, finish the rest of his pregame preparation, run through his warm-up in the bullpen and then go out and reinforce that the kid who stood tall and won the clinching game of the 2007 World Series in Colorado for us was not to be messed with in October.

He moved his fastball around the strike zone as if using his own personal, hidden joystick on the mound. His changeup danced and his curve broke on command. But it was the cutter that was his most potent weapon on this memorable evening. Well, ahem. Aside from his mind.

In control from the very first pitch, Lester retired Carpenter, the leadoff man, on a routine ground ball to shortstop. He annihilated Beltran on four pitches, throwing a cutter for strike three that broke sharply down as the helpless Beltran futilely swung through it. Though a Matt Holliday ground ball found a hole in the infield for a base hit, Lester induced a harmless pop up to Dustin Pedroia at second base for the final out of the inning.

Little changed the rest of the night. Inside, outside, up, down, Lester moved the ball around the zone and kept the Cardinals guessing. He fanned four Redbirds in the first three innings. Things got a little dicey in the fourth when Jon Jay drew a leadoff walk and, after

Lester whiffed Holliday on a lollipop 75 m.p.h. curveball that completely baffled the outfielder, Allen Craig and Yadier Molina stroked back-to-back singles. No matter. Up next, David Freese, whom Lester schooled with a called third strike on a cutter that caught the outside corner of the plate in the second, bounced right back to Lester, who started a 1-2-3 double play. While I'll resist the temptation to say Game 1 was as easy as 1-2-3 for Lester because I know better, he sure made it look that way.

How proud was I, and everyone associated with the Red Sox? This tall, quiet and earnest left-hander who was so lost nearly four months earlier in Oakland now commanded this World Series. He threw 7.2 shutout innings as we opened with an 8-1 statement rout. He held St. Louis to five hits while striking out eight and walking just one. When he walked off the mound to a standing ovation with two out in the eighth, he had become the first pitcher to toss seven scoreless innings in Game 1 of a World Series in twenty-four years, doing something nobody had since Cincinnati's José Rijo against Oakland in 1990.

Five days later, with the Series even at two games apiece, Lester and Wainwright were matched against each other again, this time in St. Louis's Busch Stadium. And again, Lester was on point. Onto his 7.2 shutout innings from Game 1 he tacked three more to start the game. Entering the St. Louis half of the fourth, the Red Sox led a 1-0 nail-biter and Lester had 10.2 consecutive scoreless World Series innings in the bag. Then, after throwing a called third strike past center fielder Shane Robinson, he left a 1 and 0 fastball over too much of the plate, and Holliday launched a rocket sailing over the center-field fence.

In the white-hot spotlight of the big stage, this was one of those fork-in-the-road moments where a true ace emerges, and lesser starters maybe begin to feel their vulnerability and unravel. Swing game of a 2-2 World Series, score now 1-1, Wainwright far sharper than he was in Game 1 (he would strike out ten and walk only one in his seven innings), the 47,436 packing Busch Stadium smelling blood and a bad moon rising. On the mound, Lester toughened. He breathed. Breathed deeply . . . in through his nose . . . filling up his lungs fully . . . exhaling through his mouth. And instead of dwelling on the one mistake he had just made over two World Series starts, he locked right back into the moment. Without question, this was a different man than the uncertain guy who was searching back in Oakland in July. He threw a good backdoor cutter for a called strike one to the next hitter, Beltran, followed that with a fastball out of the zone but then, on his third pitch, induced a fly ball to left field. Then, in another three-pitch at-bat, Molina scorched a liner that a leaping shortstop, Stephen Drew, snagged to end the inning.

Though the Beltran and Molina balls were hit hard, Holliday's homer was the only egregious mistake Lester would make—at least, the only one for which the Cardinals made him pay. In the dugout after the fourth, Lester regrouped, drawing upon his now steely mental skills and the always insightful advice of David Ross, who had become Lester's personal catcher that season and, in times of difficulty, shrewdly and consistently reminded the six-foot-four lefty to stay tall with his posture so as to work from a downhill angle. From there, Lester breezed through three consecutive 1-2-3 innings, the fifth, sixth and seventh, retiring eleven consecutive Cardinals. Finally, with two out and a man on second in the eighth, with the Sox leading 3-1, manager John Farrell summoned closer Koji Uehara to obtain the final four outs. Over 7.2 innings, Lester struck out seven Cardinals while walking zero. Holliday was the lone St. Louis player to draw blood. Over two World Series starts and 15.1 innings, Lester was 2-0 with an 0.59 ERA. He had positioned us to win it all, he was so dominant.

Two frequent companions during a baseball season, joy and exhaustion, accompanied the charter flight back home where, two days later, on October 30, John Lackey would rise to the occasion on the mound, Shane Victorino would drive home four runs and we would win our third World Series title in a ten-year span. Never have I been a part of a World Series champion team as a player. The closest I came was with those 1996 Padres, when I started the NL West–clinching game in Los Angeles on the last day of the season before we were swept by St. Louis in an NL Division Series. But I can safely say, with full insider knowledge, that whenever you are associated with a World Series win in any capacity, it is absolutely awesome. There I was in the stands as Game 6 moved toward a crescendo with Uehara on the mound in the ninth inning, and when he breezed through the ninth inning of a 6-1 game with flair—fly balls to left field from Jay and Daniel Descalso, then closing a seven-pitch Carpenter at-bat by firing an 80 m.p.h. splitter for strike three for the clincher—I hurried down to the clubhouse to join the celebration.

It was a moment I will never forget for many reasons, chief among them being the bond Jon and I developed that year beginning in that small room in the Oakland Coliseum. Together, since then we had taken many steps on a path filled with obstacles, pressure, uncertainty and hard work. And rarely is the reward this obvious, this raucous. Again, the entire city of Boston was alight. "Dirty Water," ("I love that dirty water, oh, Boston you're my home!") cued up in the ballpark, that beloved old standard from the Standells, along with "I'm Shipping Up to Boston" from the local favorites, the Dropkick Murphys. Duck boats were readied for another parade.

I rushed into that roaring clubhouse, and I can still see Jon in his soaking-wet Red Sox uniform, Oakley goggles wrapping around his eyes, cap on backwards, bull-rushing me with a champagne bottle ready to erupt in full volcanic fury. When he unleashed that cork, a spray of bubbly from the icy green bottle saturated every part of my body, soaking through my clothes straight through to my skin, and burning my eyes. I still remember him clutching that big bottle in his left hand as we hugged. Then, he moved along in search of another victim for soaking.

What neither one of us knew at the time, what we *couldn't* know at the time, was that this would be our last triumphant ride together— but not the last triumph, and far from the end of our relationship. Bonds develop between teammates, teammates and coaches and within organizations filled with people who spend a crazy amount of time together for nine months every year. Bonds that cannot be fully explained with words, but even years later are still absolutely and fully felt.

By the next season, 2014, I would take a brief leave from the organization for a new opportunity in a mental skills position with the Major League Baseball Players Association. And, on July 31 of that summer, embroiled in a contract standoff as Lester zoomed toward potential free agency, the Red Sox traded him to, of all places . . . drum roll, please . . . Oakland. Yes, baseball is amazing. You cannot make this stuff up.

That winter, following a two-month stint with the Athletics in which he went 6-4 with a 2.35 ERA in eleven starts before Oakland lost a heartbreaking 9-8, twelve-inning wild-card game (the game in which Lester's problems throwing to first became widely known and Kansas City unleashed its running game), Lefty did become a free agent and was wined and dined especially hard by the Cubs, the San Francisco Giants and, thinking they had the home-field advantage and could tug on Jon's emotions, the Red Sox. It was also during this time that I agreed to return to the Sox, and it made me feel really good when I learned months later that as part of their recruiting pitch, the Sox quietly told him that it hadn't been made public yet, but that I would be returning to the organization.

However, by failing to reach a deal while they still employed him and could box out rival clubs, the Red Sox made a strategic blunder.

They underestimated the fact that, now thirty, Lester no longer was that shy, impressionable kid they first met and employed years before. Now he was a seasoned pro, brimming with confidence and married with two children (and a third child would be born in the winter of 2016–2017). His time in Oakland revealed to him that there was life outside of Boston. And a certain former GM in Boston, Theo Epstein, a man who knew Lester exceptionally well and respected him immensely, was running the show on the north side of Chicago. In the end, Lester, with two World Series rings already, was very attracted by the lure of becoming part of a core who could deliver a World Series title to a Cubs organization that hadn't won since William Howard Taft was president of the United States in 1908. His body of work that included, to that point, six seasons of two hundred or more innings, and his now solidified reputation as a big-game pitcher in October, earned him a six-year, $155 million contract from the Cubs.

It took only two seasons in Chicago for Lester, along with our old friend Rizzo and a supremely talented cast of young talent, to stage one of the greatest stories ever told in this game, a drought-busting World Series run that theatrically rivaled ours in Boston when we won in 2004. The Cubs' Billy Goat Curse had lasted 108 years; the Red Sox's Curse of the Bambino had endured for 86. Lester went 19-5 with a 2.44 ERA as the Cubs won, led the NL with a .792 winning percentage and finished second to Washington's Max Scherzer in the NL Cy Young voting.

And today in Chicago is not unlike yesterday in Boston for Lester. Every fifth day, before he goes to the mound, he fastidiously sticks with the imagery script that has been so beneficial to making sure he is comfortable and in a good place on the mound, even when an umpire balls a should-have-been strike or a fielder makes a key error behind him.

Before they remodeled the home clubhouse to luxurious proportions in Wrigley Field in '16, Lester would steal away into the trainer's room in the old, cramped Cubs' clubhouse, or disappear into an X-ray room that he particularly liked because it was dark and he could lay out on a doctor's table that furnished the room. Just like in the old sleep room in Boston, there on the doctor's table, he would shut off the lights, set his alarm and, twenty or thirty minutes later, wake up, finish his routine and prepare for the game.

In their newly remodeled clubhouse, the Cubs, just like Boston, have constructed a sleep room, though it is different in that Chicago's contains only two beds. Always a good teammate and not nearly as rigid as some starting pitchers on their workday, conscious of his position players, Lester often retreats to the trainer's room to do his concentration grids and imagery work, so as to allow his teammates to use those precious two beds before the game.

"I'm not a 'don't talk to me' guy on the day I pitch," he says. "I like to listen to music, and I'll have that on in the background with either wireless ear phones or [earbuds], and I'll have it loud enough to where I can hear it but still have conversations with people and not sit there being an asshole. I'll walk around with that on, and then when my time comes to get ready, I'll go find a place.

"I've played with guys who don't talk to position players on the day they pitch. I want my guys to be happy with me when we go out there, and not mad at me because I didn't listen to their music or not even say hello to them. That's the way I've always looked at it. I want my guys to be happy with me and willing to play for me and not be pissed off at me."

Along with second baseman Javier Báez, Lester was named a co-Most Valuable Player in the 2016 NL Championship Series against the Dodgers, starting two games, winning one and compiling a 1.38 ERA over thirteen rugged innings pitched. For me, watching at home in October, to see Lester named as the NLCS MVP and Andrew Miller chosen as the ALCS MVP, well, the only way I could have had a better month would have been had my Red Sox not been eliminated by Miller's Indians in the AL Division Series. Really, talk about gratifying.

Lester started Games 1 and 5 against the Indians in the World Series, the first in Cleveland, the latter in Wrigley Field. He found a quiet corner in the visiting clubhouse trainer's room in Cleveland's Progressive Field to lie down, drape a towel over his head, plug in his earbuds and push play before the Cubs' first World Series game since 1945. He knows the drill. On the road, sometimes he has to get creative.

"You don't want to be in the middle of everyone, and you don't want to be stuck in a back room where you don't wake up and you're there for a little longer than you want to be," he says.

Both the routine and the results were familiar. Though he surrendered three earned runs in 5.2 innings as the Cubs were beaten by Cleveland 6-0 in Game 1, he earned the win in Game 5 while holding Cleveland to two earned runs over six innings to help keep the Cubs alive when they were one loss from watching Cleveland steal their dream. Then, in the all-hands-on-deck Game 7, Lester worked in relief for the first time in nine years, since the 2007 AL Championship Series against Cleveland, and he responded with three innings in relief of Kyle Hendricks as the Cubs won an 8-7, ten-inning all-timer.

For Lester, just as he excels with the cutter, curve and changeup in his pitching mix, it is vital for him consistently to keep what works in his preparation repertoire, and that means whether it is before a routine June start in Seattle or a prime-time October World Series start.

"You're still going to get nervous, I don't want to take anything away from that, but you're able to control those nerves," Lester says. "I feel like you can combat it a little better than if you don't have a routine and you're kind of flying by the seat of your pants. I feel that's when things can speed up on you and you don't feel normal. I feel even since I was first called up, I've had a routine so that when the [military jet] flyby is forty-five seconds too late or the national anthem goes two minutes too long, you have things to fall back on.

"And when you do it enough, you realize, 'Hey, I don't need to throw my forty-four [warm-up] pitches, I can cut it to thirty-five, or I can throw more, and I'll be fine.' Whatever. That's worked for me, the routine of 'Okay, I'm ready to go,' and you fall back on that. Then you get into the game and you have your checks and balances. This is the report, this is what I'm trying to do. I feel it's easier to recall when you're calmer, like anything else."

Since day one with the Cubs, he regularly will visit one of the club's computer guys and have him print out fifty or so concentration grid cards at a time. He'll run through five before each start, numbers looking like crossword puzzles, shuffling them up as you would a deck of cards so he cannot memorize them, and away he'll go. The accompanying audio program is in Dropbox, so that's just a click away. Before some starts, he'll only be able to locate four or five numbers in the allotted time. Before others, he'll rattle off twenty or thirty. Day to day, the level of focus can be unpredictable and erratic. That's why practice and preparation are so crucial.

Sometimes, curiosity will pique the interest of one of his Chicago teammates, who are not as familiar with this particular mental skills drill as those in the Boston clubhouse were.

"Guys see me walk around with index cards and are like, 'What the hell are you doing?'" Lester says. "I break it down, and some guys are like, 'That's cool' and others are like, 'I don't really get that.'"

Sometimes, this reminds him of the beginning of our work together, and how the whole thing started.

"For me, Tewks got to a lot of guys in Boston at an early age and didn't force anything," Lester says. "If you want to talk about it, let's talk about it. But if you don't, let's just sit here and have a drink or have dinner or lunch, or whatever it was, and just talk. Talk about the game, about how you're feeling out on the mound, whatever it is. I think that really helped him when he got back to Boston. He knew a lot of us already, he already had that trust built in so you were able to walk up to him and say, 'Hey, man, I need to talk to you about some stuff going on at home.' You know it's confidential, nobody is going to find out about it. I think that was key. You could not only talk to him about what you were feeling in baseball, but what you were going through in life, marriage stuff, family stuff, whatever it was. You knew you could always go to him, he would help you out and it would stay there."

All of it is interconnected, isn't it? Job, family, relationships, the normal stresses that life places in front of us and says, here, here you go, deal with this. The more we can stop, think rationally, compartmentalize, prioritize and then begin the task of addressing things in a logical, organized manner, the better our odds to succeed.

"I really enjoy it," Lester says. "For me, the visualization stuff is a time when you can get into a place and shut your mind down and relax. It's such a day of anticipation [start day for a pitcher]. Plus, now I've got kids, I'm taking them to school, picking them up from school, you're doing all this stuff, you're trying to be a dad, you're trying to be a husband, and when you get to the field you've got to figure out a way to turn that off, and turn on as a baseball player. This really helps me. Back in '13, my wife was pregnant and we were dealing with all that stuff, and especially during the playoffs you're not sleeping much as it is, but we'd just had a newborn, and that twenty or thirty minutes in the sleep room for me was not only relaxation with this but time to shut down and take a twenty-, thirty-minute nap and just kind of catch up. This stuff really helps you relax and gets you locked in for being in that baseball mode."

As he says, always, he has battled to keep things from speeding up on him. He knows himself well enough now to understand that this will be a fight in which he must continue to remain vigilant. There are few certainties in this game, but this is one of them. Just when a guy thinks he has something figured out, the game will rear up and show him how little he really knows. The line of new talent and young players waiting to replace you stretches out the door, around the block, down the street, and around several more blocks after that.

Not only to reach a level of success, but to maintain that level, players must understand paths that lead to their optimal performance levels physically, fundamentally and, as more and more athletes and teams are understanding today, mentally, too. Just as you study before taking a test instead of showing up unprepared, and just as a band rehearses and plans its show in advance rather than just winging it.

The most intelligent elite athletes get this. So even though there are more days behind the wagon than in front of the horse for Lester, twelve years into his sterling major league journey, he knows and understands one important aspect contained within his career.

"It will happen this year, at some point in a regular start, I'll speed up or end up being late or whatever and you speed up your routine without even knowing it and that's when it can hurt you," he says. "All of a sudden, you're just rapid fire, rapid fire, rapid fire, and then in the game instead of thinking about one pitch and one out at a time, you're worried about just getting through the inning. It'll happen. You can't be perfect. You have different outside distractions that are going on. The more consistent you can be with it, that's where I feel you have the consistency in the season. You may have one or two blips where things sped up on you or you didn't have your stuff or whatever, but that consistency of where you're at when you get on the mound, it's there."

There on that mound, as he crunches his cleats into the clay of that day's office, be it at the Cubs' spring training site in Mesa, Arizona, or hard by the Allegheny River at Pittsburgh's PNC Park, or on another World Series stage, he will be fully prepared for his latest assignment. He will know its ins and outs, recognize landmarks along the way and understand that some moments will come easy while others will come booby-trapped with the potential for trouble, some of his own making and some not.

Many of these moments he will be fully equipped to reduce to their lone common denominator. He will slow them down . . . he will pause for a beat . . . and he will . . . breathe. He will draw in a long breath through his nose until his lungs are at full capacity. He will hold it for a beat, and then he will exhale fully through his mouth.

Six seconds. That's how long it takes to inhale a deep breath, hold and release. Six seconds to perform a concept so simple that a newborn grasps it as soon as he greets the world. Six seconds to perform an act that eventually becomes so difficult that an old man on his deathbed no longer can accomplish it.

In between, careers are built. Lives are lived. And the mind can be sharpened to dimensions maybe beyond what you ever thought possible. Breathe in, breathe out, and focus on what's right there in front of you.

Epilogue

Maybe Yogi Berra knew how vital the mental side of the game was back in the 1950s, but it has taken Major League Baseball six more decades to finally begin to truly understand its wide-ranging implications. Today, twenty-two of the thirty MLB teams employ a full-time mental skills coach, and approximately twelve or thirteen organizations have multiple individuals working for them in the mental skills area. Today, when a player begins to ponder incorporating imagery and self-talk into his game, or thinks it would be beneficial to speak with a mental skills coach, he no longer feels the need to keep it top secret, as if it's something to be ashamed of, like binge watching *The Bachelor* or a Cheetos addiction. Ever so slowly in our game, we've made progress, and my hope and thought is that progress will continue to gain traction. Once the tide begins to come in, there is no turning it back.

While there are only a total of 750 players on the thirty big-league rosters, there are more than 3,000 players stocking the minors who are trying to get there, and the moments in between range from fleeting triumphs to significant peril. And each June the MLB draft adds another thousand or so major league hopefuls to the pool of those wanting to reach—and stay in—The Show. For most players who sign a professional contract, the road to the majors is a long process. For every Mike Trout, Bryce Harper or Madison Bumgarner who reaches the majors quickly, there is a Guilder Rodriguez, who, in 2014, was called up to Texas and knocked his first big-league hit after thirteen years and 1,095 games in the minor leagues.

The game is hard, and it is not for the faint of heart.

Or, the weak of mind.

The entire *process* of professionalization is a peculiar journey that brings to the hardball world echoes of the line from the iconic Grateful Dead song "Truckin'": "What a long, strange trip it's been." Upon signing a professional contract, a fleet of young players is assigned to extended spring training, where they play morning games at spring sites in Florida and Arizona in front of a smattering of onlookers consisting mainly of scouts and the occasional parent venturing out of some distant cold-weather state to see his or her son play pro ball. Extended spring ends just before the amateur draft in June. Some players then stay for the Arizona League summer season or, in Florida, the Gulf Coast League. Some play in other short-season leagues like the New York–Penn League and the Northwest League.

As players move up the ladder, the process continues through Low Class A and then High Class A. More bus rides, more peanut butter and jelly sandwiches, more cold pizza and uniforms still damp from not being properly dried in the laundry the night before. The per diem barely covers one meal when it needs to buy three. Clubhouse dues (to cover the generic food and drink supply) take a bite out of ridiculously meager salaries and players take the poorly lit field for another night in front of a "transformer crowd." Meaning the overriding background noise inside the tiny ballpark isn't the roar of the crowd but the buzz of the electrical transformers.

Many players, who only a year or two earlier were bathed in the joy of signing a professional contract, now face the reality that they just aren't good enough to make it in the majors. Most of the time, the organization informs them of their shortcomings with release papers, but sometimes the player sees the writing on the wall. A few years ago in consecutive seasons, two pitchers at the High A level sought me out for career advice. I told both of them that based on where they were on the minor league ladder, even if everything fell into place for them (meaning if they performed well at each level to get promoted and suffered no major injuries), it would be three or four more years before they would be positioned to crack a big-league roster. And even then, if they made it through A ball, Double-A and Triple-A, there were no guarantees. One player, from Australia, was twenty-two, had signed when he was twenty and was considering a return home to attend college and get into the family business. The other, twenty-five, was a college grad who was interested in law school. Both players figured that in the time required to maybe get to the majors, they could obtain the degrees they wanted. They controlled their own destinies. Each retired midseason, and each graduated and now has a successful career off the field.

No, the game is not for everyone.

It is a shock to the system, especially early, and that shock varies in seismic activity depending upon the player. An organization that provides full-service resources, investing in all aspects of a player's development up to and, yes, including mental skills, positions itself to gain a competitive advantage in so many different ways. A player may learn behaviors and strategies to cope with the ups and downs of pro baseball that may accelerate his ascent to the major leagues.

And, conversely, a player may learn that he doesn't have the right stuff and then make the decision to get on with his life.

For those who advance past High A ball, they've hurdled one of their biggest obstacles to becoming a big-leaguer. Many evaluators believe that if a player can perform successfully at Double-A, then he's big-league material. Double-A is where you notice the funnel starting to narrow, creating a logjam of players scratching to reach the big leagues. Triple-A is an interesting place. Bus rides are replaced by plane flights, which sound great until your first 4:30 A.M. wake-up call to make a 7 A.M. flight from Omaha to Syracuse to make a game that night. Most Triple-A rosters are composed of some combination of players who are on their way up and some who are on their way out. Some may refer to it as a place where players' dreams "go to die," but for others it is one final step to having their dreams come true. Players recently demoted from the majors wonder whether they'll ever see The Show again. I know what they're going through. I was sent down seven times.

And let me tell you, they're all different. On one occasion in April 1990, I was informed that the Cardinals would be optioning me back to Triple-A at game's end, and it just so happened to be that Brett Hull and some other players from the NHL's St. Louis Blues were at Busch Stadium. Hull came into the clubhouse postgame, and this was back in the good old days before we all worried about liability and there was an ever-present keg and frosted mugs in the middle of the clubhouse. I was staying at the team hotel across the street, had nowhere to go and wasn't particularly happy with current developments. So I had a couple of beers, and Hull did, too. It wasn't long before the clubhouse was empty and me, Hull and Rip Ronan, the Cardinals' clubhouse attendant, started playing catch in the clubhouse. I was beginning a three-day hiatus because, since I was out of options, MLB rules mandated that the team run me through waivers, a process in which other clubs had seventy-two hours to claim me and if they didn't, at that point I would rejoin the Cards' Triple-A team in Louisville. I remember Brett talking about how nice we had it in MLB compared to the NHL. Before long, he lit up a cigarette and I had another beer. Not long after that, I was wearing catching gear, Rip was umpiring and Hull was doing his best imitation of a pitcher. Hully mixed some strikes among the many errant throws that bounced off the cement wall behind me, one of them breaking an illuminated Budweiser sign that had been hanging on the wall. Whoops! When our game of catch ended around two in the morning, I staggered across the street back to my hotel room. The next day I woke up with a major league hangover.

Three days later, I was back in Louisville. And today, when I speak to one of these recently cut players, those feelings and memories come rushing back, allowing me to empathize with the player, giving us some common ground that allows me to offer some words and thoughts that will, hopefully, give him that extra edge in his professional progression.

The ironic thing is, once in the majors, players begin to accumulate what's called "service time." Ironic, because the minor-leaguers who never reach the bigs essentially spend their years "serving time." Those who do reach the majors will have outlasted most of the others who were in their same draft class, living through to survive the minor league process of professionalization: failure, success, injuries, promotions, demotions, releases, trades and assorted other accomplishments and mishaps.

Every day brings something different. My first minor league spring training with St. Louis in 1989, farm director Ted Simmons, the man who would become pivotal in my own career little more than one year later against that cinder-block wall in Busch Stadium, became creative one day when it was raining. Calling for a pitchers-and-catchers' meeting inside the batting cages to at least prevent a total washout on one of those days when all the players want to do is exit early, chill at the hotel and play video games or watch movies. Simmons and the coaches were intent on emphasizing the *development* part of minor league development and were running through several aspects of the pitcher-catcher relationship when he happened to ask a young pitcher how many pitches he had.

"Four!" came the answer, with enthusiasm.

"Okay," Simmons replied in his inimitable raspy voice. "What four pitches do you have?"

"Fastball, slider, curve, changeup."

"Really? Okay, young man, here's the deal. I'll let you warm up, and when you are ready we'll see how many *pitches* you really have. If you can throw your fastball over the plate in this setting—no batter, no crowd, no score, no count—seven of ten times, I will acknowledge that you do have a fastball and one pitch, and you can put that in your back pocket."

Here, offering full visuals in this demonstration, Simmons dramatically stuffed a baseball into the back pocket of his uniform pants.

"If you accomplish this," he continued, "then you will proceed to the next pitch you say you have, and if you can throw that pitch over the plate seven of ten times, I will acknowledge that whatever pitch it is—curve, slider, change—is a pitch, and we'll continue that pattern."

Well, the young pitcher could not throw his fastball over the plate seven of ten times, but he "had" four pitches. I will never forget that day because I certainly learned a lesson. Players need to be honest self-evaluators, and after turning the mirror on myself during my time in uniform, it is a brick I use as a foundation piece while coaching players today.

The harsh reality is, the number of players who have ever played in the majors for even one day is precipitously low, just over nineteen thousand. There are more dentists in the New York metropolitan area. And of those nineteen thousand, just over two thousand lasted ten or more years in The Show.

For the minor league player who does reach the bigs, the rewards are not simply the fulfillment of a lifelong dream, but financial as well. The present major league minimum salary is over $500,000. The average annual major league salary in 2017 was $4.47 million, and each day a player spends in the majors counts toward a pension. Players are eligible to take whatever pension benefit they have accumulated starting at age forty-five. Those fortunate enough to last ten years in the majors can collect a fully vested annual pension of $200,000 beginning at age sixty-two. For those who never earn the big free-agent dollars, that pension is enormously important to financially setting up the rest of their lives. For everyone—players and clubs alike—there is so much money at stake, which begs the question, Why *wouldn't* a club want to cover all of its bases, so to speak, and ensure that every sliver of competitive advantage is discovered and mined? I believe there is no question and that's why you're seeing a bigger emphasis on mental skills today and, whatever the underlying reasons, it is long overdue.

One full year in the majors—back to that thing called service time—is 172 days. From my experiences climbing that professional ladder, I know that players at different stages of their careers fight battles unique to where they are at any given moment, both on the field and in their personal lives.

For example, major-leaguers with zero to three years of service time often have options left (meaning they can be dispatched to the minor leagues at any time), they're the low man on the ladder and often they are not sure whether they even belong. Per a longtime agreement between players and owners, a team owns three "options" on a player. When that player is placed on a club's forty-man roster for the first time, the club still has the option to return him to the minors. And regarding those three options: Each year essentially is one option, meaning in his first year, a player theoretically can be sent back to the minors multiple times, and that's just one option. Because the team still holds two more options, a player's first three years in the majors can become a roller-coaster ride of false starts and not knowing what's around the next bend. Talk about mind games.

Players with between four and six years of big-league service time typically have moved past the worry of being demoted and have established themselves as major-leaguers. However, they still can't escape the anxieties and pressures. They still have those feelings, but they may not come from sources on the field, but from off the field. Players may have started a family, which creates a new dynamic to the relationship: long-distance communication. It's also the beginning of what my wife labeled "Daddy's first day home." This is when Dad's reentry to the family following a road trip or a season messes up nap times, mealtimes and often any routine Mom has established with the kids while Dad was gone. It causes chaos until he leaves again. Players begin to realize their world doesn't revolve solely around baseball anymore. Instead, they have a family to take care of and a future to plan, both of which are determined by their performance on the field.

Players at this level haven't collected enough service time for free agency (it takes six full years to reach that plateau), so the big, lottery-winning type of money isn't there yet. But, they are eligible for salary arbitration, which means that if the player and club cannot agree on a contract, they can argue it out in front of an arbiter in the winter. The player's representative extols his virtues and the club points out all of the player's negatives while arguing why he should get the lower salary figure. In a way, it's *One Flew Over the Cuckoo's Nest*. It's crazy. This process brands the negatives into a player's psyche as if by a hot iron.

The demands of the game become even more challenging for this group because they no longer are hot prospects on their way up. Pretty much since Connie Mack was pulling levers in the dugout, this saying has been rattling around big-league clubhouses: "It's easy to reach the majors, but difficult to stay there." Well, I'm here to tell you that that's a blatant lie. It is not easy to reach the majors, otherwise, the road there would not be littered with the wreckage of millions of dashed dreams. But that second part, no question that's true. The staying is not easy. The line of young players trying to take major-leaguers' jobs stretches from Toledo to Fresno to Durham, North Carolina, and back again. As the great Satchel Paige once said, "Don't look back, something might be gaining on you."

Those beyond the six-year mark probably have had a run at free agency at least once, and the fortunate among this group cashed in and now have their financial pressures eased. But the demand to perform is as high as it's ever been, and usually riding shotgun with that demand are injury issues, sometimes nagging, sometimes significant. By this stage of a career, separations from family can become even longer. With school-age children growing older, the strain hopefully remains only mild, though it is no secret that it can become serious for those families wielding multiple suitcases and itineraries. The gnawing feeling that you're missing out on moments with them that you'll never get back grows. Plus assorted other outside demands arrive at your front door and, eventually, as physical skills begin to slow, coming to terms with the decision on when to end a playing career moves center stage.

This all happens rapid fire, by the way, every bit of it, just the way you've probably noticed your own life often moving more quickly than you'd like. Where's that doggone pause button when you need it, anyway? I think back to my own wobbly beginning in the majors, exiting my debut on April 11, 1986, with a 3-2 lead over Milwaukee after coaxing a ground ball to shortstop from future Brewers Hall of Famer Paul Molitor to start the eighth in front of 17,042.

"When he came out of the game, he got a typical Yankees ovation and he was *very* animated with his cap-tipping," Molitor explains, grinning. "I remember thinking, 'There's a rookie for you, right there.' The tipping went all the way around."

Let me explain. That spring, I had been fined in our kangaroo court for failing to acknowledge a nice ovation while coming off the field one day as I was throwing those twenty consecutive scoreless spring innings. I was a rookie and sure didn't want to draw attention to myself, so I hurried off the field and walked right into the veterans teasing (and fining) me. Dutifully, I tried to correct that in my debut in Yankee Stadium against the Brewers by being extra polite. The result with my teammates wasn't much different. In the next kangaroo court, they hit me with three different fines, one for each direction I tipped my cap (the fans to my right, the fans in front of me and the fans to my left)!

Ah yes, land mines are embedded everywhere in this game, many humorous, some not so much, all of it creating so much space for mental skills coaches to work. On so many levels, the game becomes like the memorable scuffed ball I threw near the end of my career while pitching against Tampa Bay. You have no idea where it's going, so you'd better hold on for dear life. That day, a hitter whose name now escapes me flew out to left for the second out of the inning, the ball came back around the infield and, when it eventually got back to me, I immediately felt something odd. There was a small tear in the ball, which must have been caused by the cupped bat the prior hitter had used. This cut was a beauty and there was no way I was throwing the ball out. But there also was no way I knew where it was going.

The theory in throwing a scuffed ball is to hold the scuff to the opposite side of where you want the ball to go. So I called my good friend and outstanding catcher in Minnesota, Terry Steinbach, to the mound. Steiny, of course, was appalled that I summoned him with two out and nobody on base.

"What the hell do you want?" Steiny snarled at me, good naturedly, upon his arrival.

"Look, asshole. I thought you might like to see this, because I have no idea where this thing is going," I replied, showing him the ball to give him ample warning.

"Holy shit," he said. "Okay, let's go."

I do remember that hitter: Paul Sorrento. I gripped the ball with the cut to the inside of my hand so it would go down and away from Sorrento. Sure enough, it sunk like crazy down and away, Sorrento put a funny swing on it, chopped an easy ground ball toward second and cursed me all the way down the baseline.

Sometimes, it's the other guy who curses you. Other times, you're the one doing the cursing. It's just the way this game rolls. On two different occasions, I had the chance to play with one of the most prolific base stealers of all time (and, yes, my cursing was kept to a minimum when we were teammates as opposed to when I had to worry about holding him on first base!). Yes, speaking of baselines...

Rarely, a prodigy comes along whose skills level leaves him self-sufficient—or, who appears to hail from his own planet—like Hall of Famer Rickey Henderson. Both he and I were newcomers to San Diego in what would become a very memorable summer in 1996, one in which we won the NL West over Los Angeles on the last day of the season in a showdown game in Dodger Stadium. Though I was thirty-five and hadn't started in twelve days, I started on that Sunday afternoon because our manager, Bruce Bochy, thought my grace under pressure would play big, and he was right. I pitched seven shutout innings. As for Rickey, earlier that season I was sitting on a player bus headed to the airport to start another trip and it mostly was full when he came walking down the aisle looking for a seat.

Outfielder Steve Finley was sitting in front of me, and given that he had only six full seasons in the bigs at that point and Rickey had been around for sixteen, as Finley recalls, I piped up and told Henderson: "You have tenure, sit where you want" and then razzed Fins by volunteering his seat to Rickey.

"Ten year?" Rickey practically shrieked, brow furrowing, eyes narrowing, clearly misunderstanding "tenure." "Rickey been playin' seventeen year!"

Feel free to laugh—Rickey is one of the most entertaining person-alities ever—but however you view it, he did bring up an important point. From tenure to service time, from the insecurities presented by minor league options to the family pressures that build through-out the travel and expectations of a major league season, when I was playing, we were totally on our own. Looking back, it really is sort of incredible that the support system in our game was so thin for so long. But like our culture, the game changes with time, and in so many ways, now it is so much healthier.

For more than a century, the game brooked change at a horse-and-buggy pace. Yet now, teams routinely hire assistant hitting coaches, and bullpen catchers and most even employ someone to monitor the clubhouse video feeds now that instant replay is a part of our game. The use of analytics—including pitcher spin rates, infield shifts and exit velocity—has changed the way the game is viewed on many lev-els. In the early '80s, teams began hiring strength coaches. Today, that department is formally called strength and conditioning (S&C), with most major league clubs employing two full-time S&C coaches. In recent years, organizations have added S&C coaches at every mi-nor league level, too.

With advances in S&C, changes also occurred within organiza-tional medical departments. Years ago, teams employed only two trainers to care for twenty-five players. Today, teams routinely em-ploy two or three full-time certified athletic trainers (CATs) in ad-dition to a full-time massage therapist and physical therapist. And each minor league team has at least one CAT. Teams also provide chiropractic care to players as needed.

Furthermore, many teams have nutritionists on staff helping to design pre- and postgame meals for players that are more healthy than the "comfort" food of the past, such as hamburgers, fried chicken and Philly cheesesteaks. Those are relics from a bygone era (but, ah, those cheesesteaks were sooo good!). Today, clubhouses are stocked with energy bars, fruit and assorted other healthy items.

All of this leads to the next frontier in seeking a competitive advantage, and that's the mental aspect of the game. Could it be that the field of sports psychology and mental skills coaching, which has been slowly growing since the mid-1980s, finally has become accepted and realized as an important part of improving players' performance to the degree of creating a collective competitive advantage for teams?

I believe it has. As the field continues to grow and become accepted as an important part of team culture and individual player performance, I believe that within the next few years, all major league teams will have at least one person providing mental skills services. The degree to what levels these services are provided will vary from organization to organization, but they will be better than what was in place thirty years ago, and they will be better still than what we have in place today.

Baseball has long had a saying that "you're only as good as your last game." Given that this is a game built on failure—all together now, *even the very best hitters fail seven out of ten times at the plate*—it stands to reason that constructing a strong mental foundation is more important here than in any other sport. Thoughts really do become things, and it can be damaging to suffer alone.

Rhythm and results change, both in games and in life. Concentration and focus are skills that separate the successful performers from the inconsistent. We all can come to this point via different routes and paths. The important thing is that we get there. My friend Charlie Maher, Cleveland's sport and performance psychologist, talks about how he can't believe how far we've come in thirty years in this area of the game. Me, not only do I agree, but I cannot wait to see where the next thirty take us.

As the Indians' relief ace Miller says, "In the beginning of my career, I felt like if you were seen in closed-door meetings with the psychology guy, or talking too long to him in the outfield, people would think you were losing it or having major issues. I think that's gone away, fortunately."

I only wish Coleman Griffith and Harvey Dorfman could see how far the field of mental skills in major league baseball has come, and where it's headed.

Several major league teams currently have sport-science departments whose goal is to help "fuel" the players with proper nutrition and supplements while also monitoring workloads and recovery, in an effort to find the optimal performance state for each player. Today, there is ongoing research on genetic profiling geared toward discovering genetic makeup as it relates to how best to train a player. With advances in GPS tracking, companies are offering virtual reality hitting goggles that allow players to simulate hitting against, say, Madison Bumgarner in advance of actually facing the real thing. Technology like this could one day replace pregame batting practice (which most pitchers would love to see abolished anyway!).

All of this is fascinating stuff that promises to take our game deeper and deeper into the Land of the Unknown over the next several years and beyond. But these and other technological advances still cannot belie the fact that 90 percent of this game is half mental, or, depending on how you work the math, it's *every bit* of 90 percent mental, and that aspect of performance must be addressed. You effect change from the inside out. For every skeptic, there will be ten Jon Lesters and Andrew Millers, quietly applying their mental skills in the hours leading up to a game and then dominating during it. The imagery will become sharper and sharper, the self-talk more and more positive and, one day soon, as it all happens, even the ornery Little Man will stand and applaud.

ACKNOWLEDGMENTS

Bob Tewksbury

Thank you to my parents, Shirley and Ken, for allowing me to chase my dream. To my siblings, Keith, Roxanne and Shawn, for their love and support throughout my journey. Thank you to my in-laws, Vera, Bob and Billie, Kitty, Robby and Glenham, for their love and the support they gave our family during the many baseball seasons.

To my high school baseball coach, Dave Anderson, high school principal, Bob Norton, and physical education teacher, the late JD Denham. This trio of men became father figures to me during an important time in my life, for which I will be forever grateful. To my high school sidekick, Craig Weyant, who shared my love and passion for baseball. My college roommate, John Kozak, best man, Dale Emerson, and card-playing partner, Dan Luker, for their devoted friendship and support throughout many stages of my life.

Thank you to Yankees scout Jack Gillis, who signed me, and to my pitching coaches Mark Connor, Sammy Ellis, Joe Coleman, Dan Warthan, Dick Bosman and Dick Such for helping me find ways to "trick 'em." To Cardinals staff Mike Jorgensen, Ted Simmons and Joe Torre, who believed in me when I needed it most. To traveling secretary CJ Cherre and clubhouse manager Buddy Bates and his staff, thanks for making us feel at home while playing in St. Louis.

To my "backstops," catchers Terry Steinbach, Tom Pagnozzi, Todd Zeile and others, for putting down "suggestions" behind home plate . . . and to "Big" Lee Arthur Smith, for all the wins he saved for me, a couple of which didn't even make me nervous!

To my colleagues and mentors, Norm Kaye, Len Zaichowsky, Amy Baltzell, Richard Ginsburg, Steve Durant, Laz Gutierrez and Dr. Larry Ronan. To Charlie Maher, Ken Ravizza and Harvey Dorfman, the trailblazers whose work teaching the importance of the mental game in baseball paved the way for so many others. To my colleagues in the Professional Baseball Performance Psychology Group, who will continue to promote the value of the discipline.

To the many Red Sox staff and front office personnel who gave me a chance to start a second career. Heartfelt thanks to Dan Duquette, Theo Epstein, Ben Cherington, Brian O'Halloran, Raquel Ferreira and Mike Hazen. And a big shout-out to all of the Red Sox coaches and trainers who supported my work over the years.

To my agent, Joe Bick, who is as professional as they come. To the man who repaired my shoulder, which allowed me to pitch again, the amazing orthopedic surgeon Dr. Arthur Pappas, who sadly passed away in March 2017. To my physical therapist, Mark Murray, who tirelessly helped me rehab after surgery. To John Silva, Heather Crutchfield, Elizabeth Hirshfeld and Barbara Fermin at St. Paul's School in Concord, New Hampshire, who allowed me to train in the field house in the off-season year after year. A thank you to all of my fans in the Concord, New Hampshire, area who followed and supported my career over the years.

To my book agent, Rob Kirkpatrick, whose call one cold December night rekindled this project. Thanks for your leadership and guidance to see this project to the finish line. To my editor, Dan Ambrosio, for his vision, enthusiasm and belief in this manuscript. And a heartfelt thank you to my cowriter, Scott Miller, for his incredible writing and diligence in pursuit of perfection.

To Greg Maddux, Moisés Alou, Ryne Sandberg, Mark McGwire, Tim Salmon, Brian Sabean, Fred McGriff, José Iglesias, David Ortiz, Ryan Kalish, Joe Buck, Peter Gammons and Ted Simmons for their important contributions to this book.

Special thanks to Andrew Miller, Jon Lester, Rich Hill and Anthony Rizzo for their willingness to outwardly express how important the mental game is to them and how *our* work together played a part in their success.

Scott Miller

An email quietly pops into your inbox overnight, an Italian meal is shared during spring training in Fort Myers, Florida, discussions are had, things are slept on and, soon, you're firing on all cylinders on a project that consumes most of the next two years. This book wouldn't have happened, at least not to this extent, without the cooperation and care of so many.

First and foremost, of course, I'd like to thank Bob Tewksbury—All-Star, retired pitcher, mental skills coach and friend. When that email first popped in (subject line: "any interest in writing?"), my first reaction was that, like most people these days, I was already too squeezed for time. But what I knew from covering the final two seasons of Tewks's career for the St. Paul, Minnesota, *Pioneer Press* in 1997 and 1998 was that he's a good man and he has a good sense of humor. Those are my favorite kinds people. So yeah, this was someone worth investing my most valuable resource—time—in, and I'm so glad I did. Tewks and I had a whole lot of fun and laughs along the way, and along with the serious stuff, I think that comes across in these pages. And it was somewhere near the finish line that we discovered one more thing that maybe signified we were meant to work together. Both of our wives *and* his daughter Jenna were born on Halloween. What are those odds? Boo!

The true testament to how well Tewksbury is liked and respected around the game? Every single player or former player I spoke with not only willingly answered questions, but eagerly cooperated. Enormous thanks to Jon Lester, Anthony Rizzo, Andrew Miller and Rich Hill for graciously sharing their work with Tewks and opening a window into this world, and for their consistent patience with me through multiple interviews throughout 2016 and 2017. Special thanks also to Joe Torre, Greg Maddux, Ted Simmons, Fred McGriff, Mark McGwire, David Ortiz, Ryne Sandberg, José Iglesias, Paul Molitor, Ryan Kalish, Tim Salmon, Brian Sabean and Bruce Bochy for their insights into both yesterday and today. A shout-out to the legendary Peter Gammons and Fox broadcaster Joe Buck, too, as well as Peter Chase, media-relations director extraordinaire of the Chicago Cubs, and Randy Robles at the Elias Sports Bureau, official statistician of MLB.

Our literary agent, Rob Kirkpatrick, quite simply, has the vision of a great horned owl (Google tells me they have "the best vision ever" so, Rob, if that doesn't work for you, send this back to me like you did the first couple of book proposals and we'll make sure to get it just right again!). And Dan Ambrosio, senior editor at Da Capo Press, hits all the right notes and gets bonus points for being a Philadelphia Phillies fan who thankfully is a Joe Lefebvre believer (of course Lefebvre was with the 1983 Phillies World Series team, not their 1980 Fall Classic team—thanks Dan, for that save and others). I could not imagine being in better hands as a book takes shape and is executed than we were with Rob and Dan. And, Christine Marra finetooth combed every word with the precision of a diamond cutter.

My "day job," so to speak, is at Bleacher Report, where I am blessed to be surrounded by good teammates and highly skilled pros. You know you're in the right place when your editors periodically ask about your book deadline and offer to help structure schedules so that you can meet it. To this, I owe unending thanks to Stephen Meyer and Paul Forrester, and to Mark Smoyer and Elliott Pohnl as well. Thanks also to Bill Eichenberger and Tina Sturdevant.

Big thanks also to my "kitchen cabinet" of colleagues in the baseball world who for so many years, through good times and a few less than good times, past and present, unfailingly were there with valuable professional advice and abiding friendship: Bob Nightengale, Jim Caple, Danny Knobler, Jayson Stark and Jerry Crasnick. And then there are my Michigan boys: Tim Hoffman, Dr. Dan Eby, Matt "Wildman" Miller, Sam Bellestri, Greg Althaver and Jerry Walsh, guys I've grown up with, some of whom I even lost a wedding bet to (one of many stories begging to be told). Show me friends as good as these, and you're rich beyond your wildest dreams.

My parents, Alan and Rosemary, watched a little boy learn to read on the sports sections at home in Monroe, Michigan, and have been there every step of the way as I dreamed big dreams of writing about baseball and then went out and reached for the stars. Without them, I'd be, as former Twins manager Tom Kelly would say, a lost ball in tall weeds. Thanks for everything, Mom and Dad. And love to my brother, Greg, and his family, and to my sister, Jennifer, and her family as well.

Finally, to the loves of my life, Kim and Gretchen. There simply is no thanks big enough for your patience and love while enduring the days and nights I spent locked away writing. They long ago accepted that living with a baseball writer always, always means one more phone call, one more deadline, one more radio interview, and always right in the middle of dinner or an evening together at home. To each of you, as one of the great, old pop songs coming out of our backyard SiriusXM radio goes, "My love is deeper than the deepest ocean, wider than the sky . . . brighter than the brightest star that shines every night above."

NOTES

CHAPTER 5. FEAR AND LOATHING ON THE MOUND

80 **"internalized rehearsal":** Jim Taylor and Gregory Scott Wilson, eds., *Applying Sport Psychology: Four Perspectives* (Champaign, IL: Human Kinetics, 2005).

CHAPTER 8. FROM BIRD SEED TO MIND FOOD

131 **19,000 players:** Baseball-Reference.com.

131 **roughly 483,000 boys:** Odds of a High School Athlete playing College Sports, http://scholarshipstats.com/varsityodds.html.

CHAPTER 9. MOUND GAMES AND MIND GAMES

149 **mocked the "headshrinkers":** Christopher D. Green, "America's First Sport Psychologist," http://www.apa.org/monitor/2012/04/sport.aspx apa.org.

150 **"designed to assist major and minor league players":** Chicago Cubs press release announcing their new mental skills program, February 24, 2015.

154 **"He kind of taught me the value":** Scott Miller, "The Mental ABCs of Postmodern Baseball: Searching for Every Possible Edge," Bleacher Report, May 11, 2015, http://bleacherreport.com/articles/2458725-the-mental-abcs-of-postmodern-baseball-searching-for-every-possible-edge.

155 **"We work our fielding, our throwing":** Ibid.

156 **"Teams are competing on the field":** Ibid.

157   "It's a very hard thing to train": Ibid.

166   "are not the result of deliberation": Judith S. Beck, *Cognitive Therapy: Basics and Beyond* (Gilford Press: New York, 1995), 14–15.

ACKNOWLEDGMENTS

233   "My love is deeper than the deepest ocean": Tony Hatch, "My Love."

INDEX

ABOUT THE AUTHORS

Photo by Jenna Tewksbury

Bob Tewksbury is the mental performance coach for the San Francisco Giants, after spending twelve years in that capacity for the Boston Red Sox. He has a master's degree in sports psychology and counseling from Boston University. Drafted by the Yankees in 1981, he won 110 games over a thirteen-year career (from 1986 to 1998) with the New York Yankees, Chicago Cubs, St. Louis Cardinals, Texas Rangers, San Diego Padres and Minnesota Twins, was named to the National League All-Star team and finished third in the Cy Young Award voting of 1992. Notable for incredible pinpoint control, Tewksbury had a walks-per-nine-innings rate of 1.45, with a minimum of fifteen hundred innings, which ranks no. 1 on baseball's all-time list of starting pitchers since the dead-ball era. He appeared in the movie *The Scout*, playing himself. "Tewks" lives in New England with his wife, Laura. They are the parents of a grown son, Griffin, and daughter, Jenna. Bob can be contacted via his website: www.bob.tewsbury.com

Photo by Gretchen Miller

Scott Miller is an award-winning national MLB columnist at Bleacher Report as well as an analyst for MLB Network Radio on SiriusXM and a contributor to Fox Sports San Diego television. Miller was named one of the nation's top two beat writers by the Associated Press Sports

Editors (APSE) in 2016, and one of the nation's top five columnists by the APSE in 2013 and has received numerous honors from the Society of Professional Journalists and other organizations. Previously, he was a national MLB columnist at CBSSports.com and covered baseball for the *Los Angeles Times* and St. Paul, Minnesota, *Pioneer Press*, where he chronicled Tewksbury's two seasons pitching for the Twins. Scott lives in Southern California with his wife, Kim, and daughter, Gretchen.